THE BALLOONING MANUAL
Pilots, Retrieve Crews and Observers

THE
BALLOONING
MANUAL

Pilots · Retrieve Crews · Observers

Bob & Carol Howes

Airlife

England

Nothing in this manual supersedes any legislation, rules, regulations or procedures contained in any operational document issued by Her Majesty's Stationery Office, the Civil Aviation Authority, balloon manufacturers or balloon operators throughout the world.

Copyright © 1991 The Airtour Balloon Co. Ltd.

Published in the United Kingdom by Airlife Publishing Ltd. 1991

A catalogue record for this book is available from the British Library

ISBN 1 85310 284 9

Printed in England by Livesey Ltd., Shrewsbury.

Airlife Publishing Ltd.
101 Longden Road, Shrewsbury SY3 9EB, England

THE BALLOONING MANUAL

1

INTRODUCTION

Having had a taste of ballooning, however remote, many people want to further their experience and find out all they can about this fascinating sport. 'How can I get involved?' is the common plea made to balloonists.

Not everyone who is interested in balloons wants to become a pilot. For many, the fun is in **crewing**. Indeed looked at realistically, every balloon pilot depends on a good crew to enable him to get airborne, and to retrieve him after his flight. An efficient willing crew member is a welcome addition to any team. Someone with a knowledge of crewing may also be interested in being an observer at competition balloon meets. **The Ballooning Manual** introduces would-be crew members to the joys and skills of the practical side of ballooning as well as covering many of the subjects needed by a student studying for a balloon pilot's licence.

The practical aspects of **learning to fly a balloon** can be covered in a relatively short time, if the weather is favourable, but many potential balloon pilots find the thought of having to sit written papers the most daunting task of gaining a **Private Pilots Licence or PPL(Balloon)**. I was no exception myself and must admit that, having had my first flight it then took me several years to decide to attempt a PPL, in spite of logging many hours as a pilot under training (p/ut) — years when it was always easy to convince myself that I just hadn't got the brains or the time to devote to studying books on Air Law, meteorology, navigation etc. Not wasted years however, because crewing is also a very challenging and rewarding aspect of ballooning.

Eventually I realised that a university education was not a requirement for becoming a pilot and the only really daunting experience was finding the books with the right level of information needed to cover the balloon pilot's licence syllabus.

It would have been much easier if one book could have supplied all this information, together perhaps with explanations of some of the more complicated text in CAA publications. **The Ballooning Manual** fills this gap.

However, would-be students should realise that in many ballooning situations there is often no hard cut right or wrong technique. If someone else advocates a different approach to an operation it does not mean that either of us is necessarily right or wrong. There are safe ways and less safe ways of operating balloons and we have endeavoured to promote good safe practice in every case.

Enjoy your ballooning.

Carol Howes

SECTION 1

GENERAL INFORMATION

2

BALLOON DEVELOPMENT

This book is not intended to be a history of ballooning but to understand today's hot air balloon it may be helpful to briefly consider its origins.

On **5 June 1783** the Montgolfier brothers, Joseph and Etienne, were responsible for the first hot air balloon flight. They did not however, believe that the balloon was carried aloft by hot air. They imagined that the fuels they burnt, straw and sheep's wool, contained a 'lifting gas' and named it 'Phlogiston'. The first airborne passengers were a sheep, a duck and a cockerel.

The first manned flight was made on **21 November** of that year, by Pilatre de Rozier & Marquis d'Arlandes, with a duration of 25 minutes across Paris. This flight was witnessed by Louis XVI and Marie Antoinette. The king had wanted to send up two convicts as the world's first 'test pilots' but had been persuaded against it by Rozier who wanted that distinction.

The excitement of man's first flight in a hot air balloon was perhaps overshadowed only a few days later by the first flight of Professor Charles's hydrogen balloon.

On **27 August** the following year, **1784**, James Tytler made the first hot air balloon flight in Britain with his balloon 'The Grand Edinburgh Fire Balloon'. This was from the Comedy Gardens in Edinburgh.

Also in 1784, on **15 September**, the first balloon flight was made in England, when Vincent Lunardi took to the skies from the Honourable Artillery Company's grounds in London. This was with a gas balloon.

The first Englishman to fly was James Sadler. His flight was made from Oxford in a gas balloon, on **3 October 1784**.

Obviously there were difficulties in finding a suitably efficient fuel to provide the heat for a hot air balloon and having to carry a large quantity of straw or wool to fuel the braziers was not really practical. Development therefore concentrated on the hydrogen balloon. Gas ballooning became and remained very popular until the introduction of the aeroplane in the early 1900s.

Hot air balloons needed an efficient, easy to carry source of heat. During the years 1900 to 1932 Louis Godent carried out experiments with petrol burners while Piccard & Hay Cosyns explored the possibilities of using propane with no great results, and it wasn't until Yost and Piccard invented their propane burner that the forerunner of today's hot air balloon was born.

1959 saw the formation of Raven industries by Yost & Piccard who were funded by the US Office of Naval Research to carry out experiments into the feasibility of the use of hot air as a lifting medium. Their development of the propane burner was to reawaken interest in hot air balloons. The prototype balloon, which had its first flight on **22 October 1960** at Bruning in Nebraska, was a one-man affair with a crude seat arrangement. An early modification was to the burner valve which required twenty-two turns to fully open and twenty-two turns back to fully close! A quick on/off valve was soon fitted.

Modern hot air ballooning took off in the UK with the arrival in 1966 of a Piccard balloon named 'Red Dragon'. Registered G-ATTN, its first flight was from Weston on the Green in August of that year.

The first successful British built balloon was G-AVTL the 'Bristol Belle' which had its first flight in July 1967, also from Weston on the Green.

Since then various refinements have been put into practice but the basic balloon and burner systems remain very much as they were in the 1960s and a modern **Hot Air Balloon** is still relatively simple in its design and controls.

(Bob Bennett)

Fig. 2–1   'Griffin' G–BDWO, author's original home-built balloon

3

BALLOON TYPES

Special balloon shapes aside, there is a wide variety of types and sizes of balloon. The basic tear-drop shape is apparent in most types and it is in the construction and design of the gores or segments which make up the balloon, that the differences occur.

(Cameron Balloons)

Fig. 3–1   Bulbous gore envelope — Cameron Viva 90

Bulbous gore
Generally consisting of 8–12 vertical bulbous gores, with varying degrees of curvature, this type of envelope has a 'pumpkin' appearance. Each gore is built up of specially shaped horizontal panels. This design has little

horizontal stress thereby producing a very efficient envelope. The twelve gore version is suitable for artwork but the more bulbous eight gore type does not present such a good surface for intricate designs, unless they can be contained within one gore.

(Thunder & Colt)

Fig. 3–2   Smooth gore envelope — T&C

Smooth gore

This design usually consists of many narrow gores with very little curvature on each. The number of gores varies from manufacturer to manufacturer but can range from twenty to thirty-two, or thereabouts. This produces a smooth flatter surface where the higher stresses make it a little more prone to damage, but produce a better surface to carry intricate artwork.

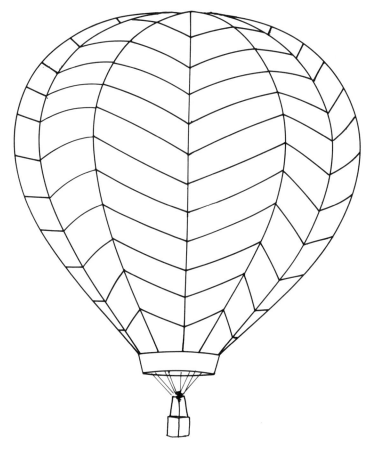

Fig. 3–3 'Diagonal' gore envelope

Diagonal cut gores
Built in America this design gives shape to the gores by using fabric on the bias. It is a style which gives rise to some very attractive diagonal colour patterns.

Straight cut gores
Another design from America with alternate gores being of completely straight runs of fabric, thus making it quick and easy to manufacture (Fig. 3–4).

Balloon sizes
In the UK the **size** of a balloon refers to its **volume** in thousands of cubic feet.

'77' refers to a volume of 77,000 cu ft.
'31' refers to a volume of 31,000 cu ft.

There is also an international classification of hot air balloon sizes.

Class	Volume	(up to)	Can carry
AX3	400– 600 cu metres	(20,000 cu ft)	1 person in harness
AX4	600– 900 cu metres	(31,000 cu ft)	1 person
AX5	900–1200 cu metres	(42,000 cu ft)	1–2 persons
AX6	1200–1600 cu metres	(56,000 cu ft)	2 persons
AX7	1600–2200 cu metres	(77,000 cu ft)	3–4 persons
AX8	2200–3000 cu metres	(105,000 cu ft)	6 persons

When deciding what type of balloon is the best for you there are several factors to take into consideration.

For many people **cost** is probably one of the most important factors. However, there are several ways of reducing this in terms of personal

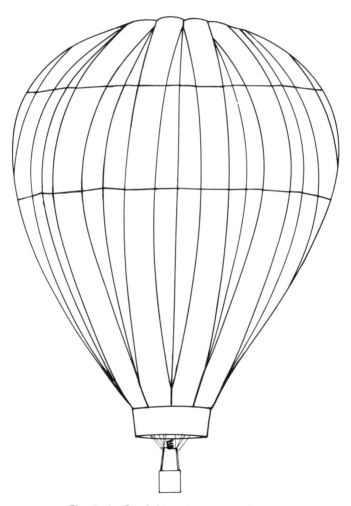

Fig. 3–4   Straight-cut gore envelope

expenditure. Taking on a partner to share the expenses, or joining together with three or four other enthusiasts to form a syndicate are popular methods.

Another way is to find a company willing to offer full sponsorship i.e. a company who will buy the whole outfit for you to fly if the envelope bears the company colours and/or logo. Alternatively, a company may be persuaded to purchase advertising banners to fit onto an existing envelope and/or basket and be willing to pay some costs, such as the annual insurance or fuel bills in return for their name being seen in the air. There are several variations which may be worked out on this theme with an interested company.

You may opt to buy a second-hand balloon 'to learn on', but do be sure you know what you are buying. It is advisable to have the balloon checked over by a BBAC inspector even if it has a current certificate of airworthiness, and never buy without seeing it inflated even if there is no opportunity to fly in it. If the balloon has been stored for any time or if it has high hours insist on a fabric test to check fabric strength, and check its porosity by trying to blow through the material. A second-hand bargain can become an expensive purchase if top panels need replacing due to weakness or porosity, and an owner may be quite unaware of any problem if the balloon has not been flown for some time.

If there is no hurry, and you have the courage and determination then building your own balloon is another direction to investigate. It is not a task to take on without being very sure of what you are doing, but by talking to other home-builders and learning the pitfalls to avoid, it could become a reality.

The **design** of balloon chosen should be considered along with other factors. With any size of balloon a multi-gore type will usually be heavier to handle than one with fewer gores, have you enough strong crew to cope with this? The choice of design could also be dependent on the amount of artwork or colour schemes being considered. Large detailed areas will look better on a smooth finish. Simple bold designs can look better on bulbous surfaces.

The **volume** best suited to your needs will depend not only on the number of people you wish to fly, but also on the number of ground crew available. Although ballooning is called the 'lighter than air' sport once the balloon has landed and needs carrying across the odd field or two this becomes an absolute misnomer, and a large or heavy balloon needs far more crew to handle it than a 'family sized' 56 or 77 thousand cubic feet balloon.

It is also worth bearing in mind that a multi-gore design envelope may in some cases cost more for repairs, especially where there is burn damage at the mouth of the balloon. Because of the small gores it is rare that a burn will be limited to one panel and chances of load tapes becoming damaged are therefore higher too.

Another consideration which may have an influence on the size of balloon chosen is the means of transport available. Some people like to keep all their equipment in a trailer while others prefer to commit themselves to another vehicle such as a van of some description. In any case the basket must be of such a size to fit the transport or vice versa.

Where will the equipment be housed when not in use? Is there the extra garage space or parking space available? If a trailer has to stand out in the open will it be weatherproof? Can the flight cylinders and propane be stored safely? (See Chapter 26: Propane Handling.)

Whatever balloon you decide fits your needs, it can be helpful to attend balloon meets to actually see the various types and to talk to people and get their opinions.

Fig. 3–5   Airtour 77 — 12-gore envelope

4

PILOT TRAINING REQUIREMENTS

The Civil Aviation Authority (CAA) oversees all flying in the UK, but the British Balloon and Airship Club (BBAC) is the governing body of the sport and on behalf of the CAA appoints instructors and examiners for the training and examining of student pilots.

UK PPL (Balloons & Airships) — rating: **Free Balloons, hot air filled**.
Fitness requirements
All that is necessary as far as a certification of fitness is a self declaration, made on form FCL150/AB (available from the BBAC) which is then countersigned by the applicant's general practicioner.
This has to be renewed every five years for applicants 39 (and under)
two years for those 40–49
one year for those 50–69
six months for those 70 (and over)

A **certificate cannot be issued** to anyone suffering from:– epilepsy, fits, severe head injury, recurrent fainting, giddiness or blackouts, high blood pressure, coronary artery disease, insulin controlled diabetes, any psychiatric disorder or any other disorder liable to cause incapacitation.

Normal colour vision is not a necessary requirement for a balloon PPL.

The certificate states that if spectacles are worn, a 'readily accessible spare pair' must always be carried.

A licence holder who through illness or injury cannot fly for twenty days or more must advise the Civil Aviation Authority in writing. Their medical certificate is invalid until they can be certified medically fit again. (The same applies to a woman pilot who has reason to believe she is pregnant.)

In spite of its 'champagne image' balloon flying and alcohol should not be mixed. No pilot should fly when under the influence of alcohol or any drugs which could impair his performance. Small quantities of alcohol in the bloodstream can affect flying performance, suppressing the body's normal reaction to 'danger' which produces an acute state of 'alertness'. High altitudes with less available oxygen can serve to magnify this impairment. Research has shown that even 40 mgs of alcohol per 100 ml of blood (a double whisky or a pint of beer) resulted in an increase in errors by both experienced and inexperienced pilots. A minimum interval of eight hours between alcohol and flying is a general recommendation, but the effects of a large intake of alcohol can still be apparent after twenty-four hours.

Various medications can also affect flying performance and it is wise to check with the doctor before taking any prescribed medicines. Even common proprietry medicines could affect performance. If in doubt, a trial dosage over twenty-four hours prior to flying is advisable.

Twenty-four hours should also be allowed to elapse following an anaesthetic, even local or dental ones.

It is recommended that active pilots do not donate blood since it can take several weeks for the circulation to return to normal afterwards.

Practical requirements

Sixteen hours flying experience spread over six or more flights is now the minimum acceptable air time. Two flights are required to be with a BBAC approved Instructor while others may be with any other licensed balloon pilot. It is recommended that the instructing pilot has a minimum of ten hours as P1. It is worth noting that the sixteen hours flying experience is a minimum time and generally a student will take an average of twenty hours to reach the required standard.

A student pilot must record all flights in a pilot's log book and also a BBAC Training Record book. Both should be signed by the instructing pilot. The Training Record is a more detailed log of the flying exercises and training carried out with comments from the instructing pilot for the benefit of both the student and the next instructing pilot.

A student pilot is also required to attend a BBAC 'Landowner Relations' course.

Age requirement

Seventeen years is the minimum age at which a student pilot may take a flight test.

Examinations

There are three **written** examination papers composed as follows:–

Aviation Law
Twenty questions with multi-choice format.
Time allowed — thirty minutes.

Airmanship & Balloon Systems
Thirty questions with multi-choice format.
Time allowed — forty-five minutes

Navigation & Meteorology
A two part paper.
Part I. Navigation.
Eighteen questions (not multi choice format)
Part II. Meteorology.
Twelve questions with multi-choice format.
Time allowed — two hours

The pass mark for all papers is 70%.

There is no negative marking for wrong answers (i.e. no points are given for a wrong answer but no other points are deducted).

A new subject **Human Performance and Limitations** is being introduced to the PPL syllabus (applicable to all categories — including balloons and airships) and a pass in this subject will be requirement for all private pilot licences issued or re-issued on or after **1 January 1992**.

The examination paper will consist of twenty questions with a multi-choice format and a time allowance of twenty minutes. The pass mark will be 70%.

The subjects covered by the syllabus come under four main headings:
- Basic Aviation Physiology and Health Maintenance
- Basic Aviation Psychology
- Stress, Fatigue and their management
- The Social Psychology and Ergonomics of the flight deck

At the time of publishing, the Navigation paper is also under review and will probably appear in the future in a multi-choice format.

Flight Test
This is a flight taken with a BBAC appointed examiner.

To qualify for this a student must be recommended as having reached the required standard by a BBAC Instructor and must also have successfully completed the written examinations.

Solo Flight
Having satisfactorily completed a flight test, a solo flight under supervision — either by the examiner or an instructor delegated by him — is necessary before a licence can be applied for. The solo flight has to be a minimum of thirty minutes duration.

Extensions to a PPL
Commercial Balloon Pilots Licence: CPL(B)
This licence came into being with effect from 1 January 1989. It is a requirement for pilots undertaking public transport flights and aerial work flights. A **CPL(B)(restricted privileges)** enables a pilot to undertake aerial work flights only.

Display Authorisation
At present a PPL holder has to satisfy a CAA appointed balloon display evaluator as to his/her ability to tether a balloon competently and safely. Their approved application is then submitted to the CAA.

There was no charge at the time of publication, but the whole system is currently under review by the CAA, together with the scale of fees to be introduced.

Night flying rating
To gain this a pilot has to make two night flights with a suitably rated instructor and be recommended by the instructor for the rating. Night flying in a balloon isn't a case of taking off at dusk and flying until sunrise. Not many balloons can remain airborne for that length of time and of course navigation is quite difficult in the dark. All this rating really enables a balloon pilot to do is to fly out of a take-off site a short time before sunrise.

Instructor Rating

Instructors are appointed by the BBAC Panel of Examiners. Candidates are required to have had at least fifty hours experience as Pilot-in-charge over a minimum of two years as a balloon PPL holder. They also have to take part in a two-day instructor course and take another flight test with an examiner. A good safety record is another important factor for the panel to take into consideration. To maintain the rating an instructor has to attend a two-day course every two years.

FAI Sporting Licence

This is a licence any UK PPL (Balloons and Airships) can apply for. It enables a pilot to take part in international meets and competitions. The Federation Aeronautique Internationale (FAI) issue the licence through the BBAC.

Radio Telephony Rating

This rating is needed to operate a VHF radio in the balloon. The Civil Aviation publication CAP 413 contains the R/T procedures for the private pilot. Examinations and tests for the **Flight Radiotelephony Operators (restricted) Licence** are held at various centres by CAA appointed examiners. The examination consists of a written test, with multi-choice answers and a practical communications test. For the practical communications test a candidate has to carry out a simulated cross country flight which includes emergency and airways procedures.

Aircraft radios, even non-installed hand-portable types require a licence. Aircraft radio licences are issued by the Aeronautical section of the Radio-communications Agency of the Department of Trade and Industry.

BBAC Membership

Although this is not a compulsory requirement for a balloon pilot, it is to be recommended. As well as receiving the club's magazine, **AEROSTAT**, all known holders of UK PPL (Balloons and Airships) are sent **Pilots Circular** free of charge. Student pilots may also receive this on request. *Pilots Circular* maintains an updated listing of sensitive area information together with reports from the Flying Committee and Technical Committee to keep pilots abreast of all the current changes in ballooning and air law, plus many other items of interest.

BBAC members do not have to pay a fee for the annual CofA renewal on a non-commercial balloon.

Membership of a local BBAC Region will keep a pilot abreast of news and events in his area. Details of local regions will be found in the Aerostat magazine. Some regions organise ground schools for student pilots, R/T courses and technical lectures.

CREW REQUIREMENTS

When a student pilot presents himself for a flight test, he/she has to provide sufficient crew for launch and retrieve. However, for this and any other flight it is not just the 'quantity' of crew which is of importance but also the 'quality' — i.e competence and experience of crew members.

Physical fitness
Although ballooning is classed as a 'lighter than air' sport it can prove to be just the opposite. It is surprising how heavy everything can become, for example when all the equipment has to be carried from the landing place to the retrieve vehicle, even over a relatively short distance. All crew members therefore need to be fit and able to do heavy lifting when necessary.

As crew will discover, especially if flying at balloon meets or competition events, they will also need the stamina to get up at the crack of dawn, go long periods without food, unpack, pack up and refuel the balloon several times in the day, get to bed very late and repeat the exercise the next day; all the time remaining alert and cheerful. By the last day of a week's competition a crew has really got all this down to a fine art!

A willingness to receive telephone calls at the crack of dawn and the ability to arrive twenty minutes later at a launch site fully clothed and awake are helpful qualities to be found in crew members.

Driving Licence
Not essential for every crew person but at least one member of the crew has to be able to drive the retrieve vehicle. A careful driver, able and willing to drive a wide variety of cars and vans is a great asset to a crew.

Map Reader/Navigator
A person able to read and interpret an Ordnance Survey 1:50,000 scale map is another invaluable crew member. Not only is this person an asset on the ground, navigating for the driver of the retrieve vehicle, but many pilots like to fly with a good map-reader to help with navigation in the air, especially in competition flying. A good map reader may be able to fulfil the other requirements necessary to be an Observer and take part in balloon competitions.

All crew members should have a good knowledge of the BBAC: Pilot code of conduct. (Chapter 20 Landowner relations.)

Balloon meets
Crew members who are not necessarily attached to a balloon at a meet may like to volunteer to assist with some of the non-flying tasks. Most meets require a Safety Officer, Met. Officer, Landowner Relations Officer, Launch Master and numerous other people to help with booking-in arrivals, retrieve telephone, refuelling, catering, etc.

BBAC membership
Crew members can benefit from membership to both the BBAC and their local region. The *Aerostat* magazine and Regional newsletters will have articles of interest and also details of balloon meets to be held locally, nationally and internationally. Local regions will certainly appreciate offers of help when holding meets and usually have regular evening meetings, when potential crew members have the chance to get to know local pilots. Regional meetings may just be social get-togethers or there may be guest speakers on balloon related subjects, training sessions, or technical lectures. Training courses for student pilots and crews are often organised at local region level.

5

THE BASIC BALLOON

The main components of a balloon are the envelope, burner and basket.

The **envelope** is made up of a number of vertical gores, each one consisting of several panels of fabric sewn together. In a 12 or 8 gore balloon the panels are cut horizontally, whereas in a multi-gore envelope the panels generally run vertically. The most common fabric used is rip-stop nylon with a polyurethane (p.u.) coating. Early fabric had a crisp p.u. coating, but modern fabrics now have an easier to handle, soft coating. Ripstop comes in several weights, generally from 1.5 to 2.5 oz/sq m. The heavier the fabric, the heavier the balloon will be, but heavier fabrics can

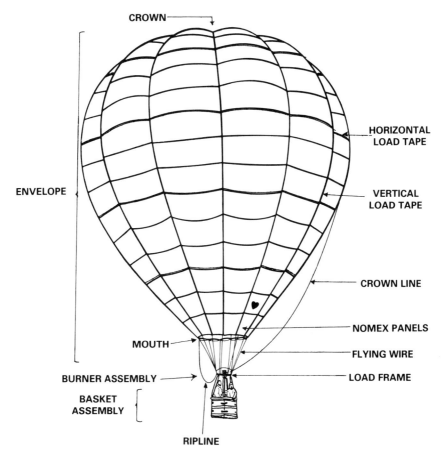

CROWN

HORIZONTAL LOAD TAPE

VERTICAL LOAD TAPE

ENVELOPE

CROWN LINE

NOMEX PANELS

MOUTH

FLYING WIRE

LOAD FRAME

BURNER ASSEMBLY

BASKET ASSEMBLY

RIPLINE

be harder wearing. The base of the envelope usually has panels of **Nomex** fabric. This is a flame proof material and can withstand the occasional lick from a burner flame. A scoop or skirt which hangs below the mouth of the envelope is usually made of Nomex too.

The weight of the balloon is borne by the strong vertical webbing tapes, or **vertical load tapes** which run from a ring at the top of the envelope, the **crown ring**, down to the mouth, where the load is then transferred to stainless steel **flying wires**. There are also hoops of tape known as **horizontal load tapes**. These help to take horizontal stresses and would in an emergency act as a 'rip-stop', preventing vertical tears from extending.

The **crown line** is a rope which is attached to the crown ring and is used during inflation.

Most modern envelopes employ a **parachute venting system** which is simply a parachute sitting inside a hole in the top of the envelope. In flight this is held in position by the internal pressure of the envelope. Operation of the **rip line** pulls the parachute down into the envelope thereby venting hot air to control vertical movement of the balloon. When the rip line is released the parachute reseals.

There are still some older balloons flying with **Velcro ripping systems**. Instead of a parachute there is an opening around a portion of the top of the envelope which is sealed before flight with a wide band of Velcro. Operating the **rip line** opens the Velcro enabling the balloon to land. The Velcro rip is not designed to reseal so in order to vent small amounts of

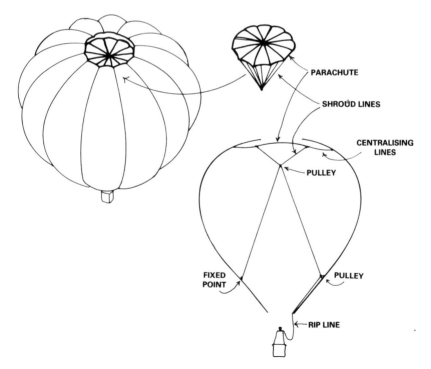

PARACHUTE

SHROUD LINES

CENTRALISING LINES

PULLEY

CENTRALISING LINES

FIXED POINT

PULLEY

RIP LINE

Fig. 5–2   Parachute ripping system

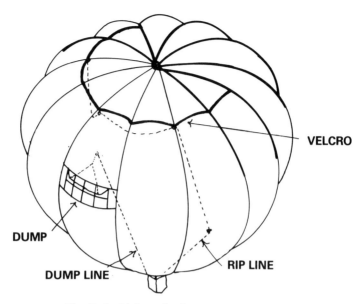

Fig. 5–3   Velcro ripping system

heat in flight these balloons also have a **dump valve** on or about the equator which is a self-closing panel operated by means of another control line known as the **dump line**.

Some envelopes have other control lines to operate rotation vents. These vents, usually two diametrically opposite one another on the sides of the envelope, as their name suggests cause an envelope to rotate when

Fig. 5–4   Burner assembly (T&C Burner: Airtour frame)

held open. They are mostly found on larger public transport balloons.

The **burner** sits in a frame which connects to both the basket and envelope. Constructed from stainless steel a burner can consist of single, double or multiple coils. The number depends on the size of envelope to be heated. A pilot light burner is generally situated within each coil. The burner and pilot light control valves are fitted beneath the coils together with the burner pressure gauges. Fuel hoses connect the burner and pilot light valves to the propane flight cylinders. When the balloon is on the ground the burner is held above the basket by a set of four nylon **support poles**.

The balloon **basket** is a woven cane or willow construction. Various alternative materials have been tried but nothing has matched the woven design and natural materials for shock absorption, durability and cost. The top rim of a basket is usually padded and covered with suede or leather, often with matching leggings to cover the support poles. The base rim is generally covered with hide to protect the weave when landing. The floor of a basket can either be woven or a heavy duty plywood. The stainless steel basket wires pass down through the weave, cross the underside of the basket floor and then up through the weave of the opposite wall, effectively forming a sling to take the basket weight. These wires are protected on the base of the basket by wooden runners.

The **fuel cylinders** strap into the basket for flight. There are holes in the weave to take the straps. Cylinders can be stainless steel or aluminium. The number carried will be dependent on the size of cylinder, size of balloon and the expected duration of the flight. There are two basic types of cylinder. Master cylinders have a liquid propane outlet valve for a main

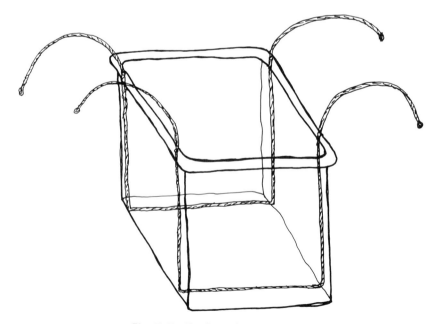

Fig. 5–5   *Basket wire assembly*

burner hose and a vapour outlet valve for a pilot light hose. Slave cylinders only have a liquid propane outlet valve. It is sensible to have padded covers on cylinders. These not only protect cylinders from exterior damage but also protect the basket occupants from bruises if they collide with a cylinder on landing. The insulation provided by a cover can also play a part in keeping a heated cylinder warm in winter flying conditions.

Of course to fly a balloon there are many necessary items of equipment to be added to this basic balloon outfit. A few, not so necessary, items can also make ballooning easier or more comfortable. Ballooning equipment is covered in the following chapter, Chapter 6.

6

BALLOONING EQUIPMENT

Certain basic equipment is necessary in preparation for any flight and the following items include those also required when about to undertake a PPL Balloon flight test with an examiner.

Airworthy balloon. This speaks for itself. While it is not a requirement to have a balloon with a certificate of airworthiness the equipment to be used must be in good airworthy condition. Maintenance of a balloon and its equipment is covered in Chapter 24.

Inflation fan. An invaluable item of balloon equipment which cold inflates the envelope prior to using the burner for hot inflation. It usually consists of a well guarded propeller driven by a small petrol engine. Always check that there is sufficient petrol for your inflation.

Fig. 6–1   Airtour inflation fan

A **fire extinguisher** should always be kept in the basket. This should be readily accessible and checked regularly. Many balloonists keep a second extinguisher to hand when inflating. This can be one normally carried in the retrieve vehicle or trailer and can be larger in size than the one carried in the basket, because weight or space will not be such a critical factor here. Some inflation fans have an extinguisher mounted on the frame for convenience during inflation.

Fuel cylinders. Ensure that cylinders are full and that sufficient fuel is available for the intended length of flight, plus a good reserve to cope with the unexpected. There must be a master cylinder for each pilot light.

Instruments. A serviceable **altimeter** is a legal requirement to allow the balloon to be flown within the height limitations laid down by air law. The only other instrument required by air law is a **clock** or watch since the law states that take-off and landing times must be recorded. Most instrument packs also have the addition of a variometer or rate of climb and descent meter. Some also include a temperature gauge which connects to a thermister in the envelope and gives a readout of the envelope temperature in flight and the ambient temperature.

Basket holdall. A place to stow envelope bag, coats plus all those last minute items prior to landing. The Airtour Ballooning **kangaroo pouch** is ideal for the purpose. Designed to fit in most baskets, the drawstring top closure also has a flap lid with pocket to stow small items such as cameras and radios.

Back-up ignition. Most burners these days have their own integral ignition system but an alternative means of re-lighting the pilot light should always be carried. This could be matches (of the safety variety so

Fig. 6–2 Quick release

Fig. 6–3   Airtour mapboard

they will not ignite on impact!), igniters or strikers. There is a wide variety of igniters, generally sold for domestic gas appliances. Always choose one which will survive the rough treatment it can receive in the basket. Some work on a piezo-electric principle, requiring no batteries or gas refills, simply producing a spark. Others require batteries and/or gas refills and obviously need checking before each flight. If stored in tight pockets, buttons can become depressed and gas leaked away or batteries flattened. Strikers simply rely on a flint to produce a spark for ignition. Whatever is carried as back-up, ensure that you can actually light the burner with it while you are on the ground. In some cases the burner may have to be tilted to get the igniter to the pilot light. Whatever is carried should be in an easily accessible place.

Airhorn. Simply a means of telling others that you are there! It can be very useful in competition flying or when flying at balloon meets, in the presence of several balloons, since a balloon directly above is completely out of sight. Hand-held horns which operate off small canisters of compressed air are ideal, though they should be carefully stowed in the basket. (Leaning against one and setting it off unwittingly when landing can be very alarming!)

Quick release/restraint. A means whereby the basket can be fastened by a line (recommended length, up to five metres) to the vehicle for safety when inflating and which can be quickly released when ready to take off. Its purpose is to act as an additional crew member, one who is unlikely to have to let go in an emergency other than under the direct control of the pilot. **A restraint line is not a tether line**. Various mechanical devices are available to release the line, or it is possible to employ a special knot which will release when the free end of the line is pulled. A quick release/restraint line must be used on all training flights and checkouts.

Tether line. Generally more than one is needed for tethered flight along with a **V-bridle** for attachment to the burner load frame.

Handling line. This is a lightweight line or tape, coiled and stored in a bag or case with one end already attached in the basket. Its purpose is simply to guide a balloon in very light wind conditions. If, for example, a balloon was becalmed over an area where landing was not practical the handling line could be thrown down to crew who could then simply move the still inflated balloon a short distance to a more suitable place.

Maps and charts. Charts showing the airspace information should be carried for the area to be flown. The 1:500,000 ICAO chart (½ million) covers the UK in three sheets and has airspace information up to FL245. (Flight level 245 = 24,500 ft.) Lower airspace information only, up to 3000 ft, appears on the 1:250,000 (¼ million) charts. Fifteen overlapping sheets cover the country. For the benefit of pilots carrying VHF radio the frequencies required for contacting aerodrome traffic zones are printed on these charts.

Balloonists often find it easier to translate the air information on to the Ordnance Survey 1:50,000 chart since the larger scale makes navigation from these maps much simpler and more accurate. Also plotted on these maps are the sensitive areas published by the BBAC — areas where

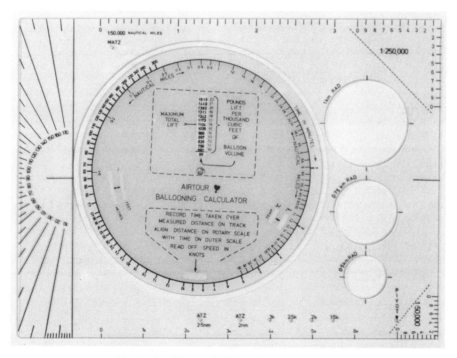

Fig. 6–4   Airtour Ballooning Calculator

landing and/or low overflying is not recommended, usually because of valuable livestock or unfriendly farmers or landowners. An Airtour Ballooning Calculator (see below) takes a lot of the guesswork out of marking up the air information and also speeds up the positioning of sensitive areas.

OS maps are also now available overprinted with air information and sensitive areas.

Pooley's Flight Guide. A compact reference giving detailed information on aerodromes, met, radio frequencies, controlled airspace and other aeronautical information. A useful addition to a pilot's flight case.

Mapboard/clipboard. Most pilots find navigation is easier if the map in use is on a mapboard or clipboard. These give a firm surface for drawing on. They should not be too large or stowing them safely on landing can present a problem. Airtour Ballooning produce an A4 size clipboard and a 22 in x18 in (560 mm x 460 mm) mapboard. Both are printed with handy pre-take-off and pre-landing check lists, together with the phonetic alphabet and some radio frequency information. The mapboard also has pockets to take a ballooning calculator and a ballooning scale.

HBM-1 scale. A 'ruler' which gives a direct read-off when measuring distances on O.S. maps, 1:500,000 and 1:250,000 charts.

A **Load chart** needs to be carried, to calculate the amount of lift available for each flight. This enables a pilot to work out the payload, or amount of fuel and passengers which the balloon can safely carry. (See Ballooning Calculator, below.)

Airtour ballooning calculator. Not a necessity, but a very helpful instrument. Used for calculating airspeed, and average flight speed it also has several other functions; feet/metres and temperature conversion

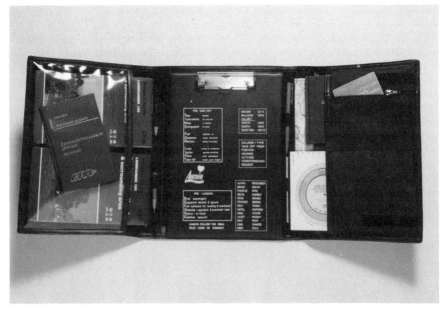

Fig. 6–5   Airtour Observer Organiser

scales; standard size sensitive area stencils with facility for drawing larger areas; means of drawing ATZ'S and MATZ's — including stubs; roamers to transpose reference points from 1:250,000 charts to OS maps; load chart and ready reckoner; protractor.

Observer/Ballooning Organiser. Padded 3-fold document case. Designed for observers but also invaluable for other balloonists. Comes complete with Airtour Ballooning A4 clipboard to hold task sheets, observer report sheets, etc.; clear pockets for maps, pockets for notebook/pilot's logbook, ballooning calculator; elastic loops for pen/pencils and HBM scale/ruler; pencil case and attachment for stopwatch or compass.

Flight bag/holdall. A bag to contain personal equipment. Many pilots and crew like to keep their ballooning kit ready packed in one bag. Airtour Ballooning have a range of suitable bags of various sizes, from a small hip pouch up to a large holdall (large enough to take flying suit, crash helmet and wellies!).

Fig. 6–6 Airtour flight bags

Chart case. Balloonists flying in different parts of the UK often have the need to carry large numbers of O.S. maps in retrieve vehicles. Since two sets of maps are needed for each area(one flying and one retrieve) and an area can require up to nine maps, it doesn't take long to overflow the cardboard box in the boot. Airtour Ballooning has a purpose-built chart case which will hold 60–70 folded maps keeping them clean and free from damage.

Retrieve vehicle. An obvious item on the list and one not easily forgotten! Points to remember are: ensure that there is petrol in the tank or that the crew know they have to find a fuel station somewhere on their travels — and also check that the retrieve driver and not the pilot has charge of the ignition keys. Another good idea is to let the crew know where the jack and spare wheel are — just in case . . . . Obviously if other people are to drive the vehicle the insurance cover must include this.

Windsock. Where a launch site is regularly used a windsock is a useful indication of the surface winds.

Crew. Having sufficient people to help makes all aspects of inflation and subsequent retrieve an easy task, providing everyone knows their expected role and that new crew members are well briefed. Too few crew and the task becomes much harder with the greater risk of damage to crew and/or other people when inflating, not to mention damage to the balloon itself.

Documents. When taking a flight test a student must be able to produce the following documents:–

> BBAC Pilot Training Record which includes a signed instructor recommendation for a test flight.
> Personal log book
> Medical certificate
> Certificate of insurance for balloon

Landing cards. The BBAC Pilot Code of Conduct reminds pilots that a landing card should always be presented to a landowner after landing on their property, giving the pilot's name and address, balloon registration and retrieve vehicle number.

Fig. 6–7   Airtour chart storer

7

CREW AND CREW BRIEFING

CREW

Clothing
It is recommended that crew members wear clothing which offers protective cover for arms and legs — especially for crew at the mouth of the balloon during inflation. Preferably, clothing should be made of natural fibres since high temperatures can cause man-made materials to melt and an accidental burn can be made a lot worse by moulten clothing adhering to skin. Oddly enough though, Nomex, one of the best fabrics for flame and heat protection is actually a man-made fibre!

An all-in-one style overall or flying suit is probably the most suitable type of garment to wear for pilot and crew alike. This has the advantage of being protection against the mud (and worse!) which can be collected in the course of inflation or retrieve, as well as being removable before entering the local hostelry or roadside cafe for the necessary sustenance after a flight.

Gloves are a sensible precaution as a protection from heat and rope burns. Again, man-made materials should be avoided where possible. Gardening or work gloves are a good idea and readily available from gardening or hardwear shops. Gloves also protect hands from the general 'wear and tear' of handling heavy and sometimes muddy equipment. Gloves should always be worn when handling propane.

Footwear should be chosen for suitability in the conditions likely to be encountered. Soles which will have a good grip on damp grass, or in thick mud are a good idea. A style which affords protection and support to ankles is also recommended.

Headgear. For pilots and passengers a protective helmet is strongly recommended. Even the most experienced pilot cannot predict his landing conditions and head injuries can be sustained so easily, often with serious results. There are several balloonists around today who either wish they had been wearing a helmet to avoid an injury or feel they owe their lives to wearing one in an unexpected situation. Nowadays there is a wide range of helmets made for other sports and recreations which are also suitable for ballooning, so the excuse that the only helmets available are very heavy motor-cycling ones no longer applies.

Crewmanship
Every pilot knows that a good crew is invaluable. It makes the whole operation of flying the balloon fun for everyone without sacrificing anything for safety, and takes some of the stress and strain off the pilot

who does not have to be continually double-checking that crew have done their allotted tasks.

All crew should be aware of two golden rules for personal safety which must apply at all times during inflation, take-off, tethering or deflation:-

- **nobody at any time should allow themselves to be lifted off their feet**. They should release their hold immediately they feel this is about to happen, whilst giving verbal warning to the pilot where possible.
- **no rope or control line etc. attached to the balloon should be twisted round hands or other parts of the body** to get a better grip. It could prove impossible to release such a hold in time to prevent personal injury if the balloon made a sudden violent movement.

It should always be remembered that whatever the emergency, a pilot inside the basket is in a far safer position than someone dangling on the outside, or hanging from the crown line or a handling line.

Anyone wishing to crew for a balloon should know that smoking is dangerous in or around the vicinity of a balloon or trailer. Cylinders do occasionally develop leaks and propane may be released when coupling hoses to tanks etc. or burner testing. Propane vapour does not quickly disperse and an explosive mixture can easily build up. It is incredible how many people will light up a cigarette without considering their proximity

Fig. 7–1   Crown line crew

to propane. Crew should be alert to spectators smoking both during the rigging and inflation of the balloon and also after landing when the pilot may vent fuel from the lines before dismantling the burner assembly.

If you are asked to crew and do not fully understand what is expected do ask questions before things get under way.

CREW BRIEFING

A good crew person is one who knows exactly what is required in whatever capacity the pilot of the balloon asks them to act. A good pilot is one who thoroughly briefs the crew. A full crew briefing should always be given prior to inflation so that everyone concerned knows the general procedure and what is expected of them in particular.

One crew member should be detailed to control the **crown** by use of the crown line. Once some hot air is put into the envelope it will roll towards the crown and if uncontrolled it will lift the crown as a bubble. It therefore needs to be held down by applying weight to the end of the crown line. Inevitably, as the envelope fills the crown will climb, but the crown line should not be treated as a tug-of-war. Rather, by maintaining a steady pull, and very slowly walking in towards the balloon, the crew person on the rope can ensure that the crown gently rises. The weight should be maintained until the pilot indicates that the envelope is ready to come completely upright and the crown line walked in, and attached to the basket. Usually no more than one person is necessary in this position unless the balloon is a large one. However it is important that the pilot is aware of the number of people holding the crown down. Often willing onlookers believe the crown line handler to be in difficulties and rush to their assistance. Holding the crown down too heavily can cause overheating if the pilot is not aware of the extra weight being applied. As soon as cold inflation commences the crown crew should be ready to steady the envelope as it lifts. The pilot should then signal to the crown crew when hot inflation is about to commence.

Two other crew should be detailed to hold the **mouth** of the balloon open to allow the pilot to commence inflation. They should be instructed to keep the underside of the mouth at ground level whilst keeping the sides out and the top up, to avoid the possibility of burn damage to the fabric. They should stand outside the wires, backs to the burner, but able to glance over shoulders at the pilot/burner to check progress. As the envelope fills so it will start to climb and the crew members can transfer their holding positions lower round the edge of the mouth. As the envelope fills with hot air it rises until the basket lifts upright and the crew should then transfer their hold to the edges of the basket to keep it in contact with the ground. Care should be taken to avoid contact with the flying wires as they may become heated during inflation. If a scoop is fitted it is helpful if the mouth crew can attach the base securing hooks to the burner-frame/carabiners as the envelope becomes upright.

A further crew member can be detailed to control the operation of the **inflation fan** under the pilot's direction and to assist with holding out and down any side panels which may be blown or sucked in, thereby

Fig. 7–2   Mouth crew

maintaining a clear passage for the the burner flame into the envelope. The pilot will indicate when the fan should be shut down. It should then be removed to a safe location so that the basket or flying wires will not become fouled if they swing around.

(Gordon Coles)

Fig. 7–3   An inflation viewed from above

Other crew may be asked to apply weight to the basket once the inflation is under way.

All crew members will be asked to hold on to the basket to keep it on the ground once their tasks are done and the balloon is upright. As the pilot commences his pre take-off checks he will put heat into the envelope to make it light and then pull the rip line to break open the Velcro tabs which held the parachute in place for inflation. Crew should be prepared for the balloon to bounce upwards as the rip line is released and the parachute reseals. When the pilot is ready to take-off two crew members may be asked to hold down the basket on their own, while the others are asked to release their hold. In this way the pilot can lift off in a controlled manner.

When a pilot has an experienced crew a **Crew Chief** may be appointed. This person may carry out much of the pre-flight preparation, and briefing and delegation of tasks to other crew members. The ultimate responsibility for these however, still remains with the Pilot in Command (PIC).

8

THE THEORY OF BALLOON FLIGHT

Why does a balloon fly? That's easy — warm air rises, but how and why?

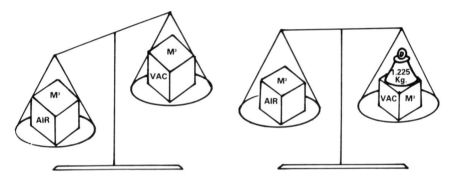

Fig. 8–1 Air is not weightless

In everyday life, the air around us does not appear to have any weight. However, if a cubic metre of air could be put on a balance opposite a vacuum of the same volume, the vacuum side would need an addition of 1.225 kg to level the balance.

Imagine the air as a fluid. A balloon in flight can be likened to an object floating in it. To be at equilibrium or buoyant, an object has to weigh the same as the amount of fluid it displaces. If there were no other influences acting upon it the object would remain stationary, suspended in the fluid.

Fig. 8–2 Buoyancy

An object weighing less than the fluid displaced will rise up through it. A heavier object will sink and "rest on the bottom" of the fluid (or sit on the ground).

For example: take a balloon with a volume of 2000 cubic metres (m^3), weighing 200 kg.

Its **total weight** would be —
>   weight of the balloon + weight of the air carried
>   = 200 kg + (2000 x 1.225) kg
>   = 200 + 2450 = **2650 kg**

However, since only 2450 kg (Volume × 1.225 kg) of air is displaced, the balloon will not fly or 'float'.

If the envelope were filled with a gas lighter than air, such as hydrogen or helium, then the balloon would weigh less than the air displaced and be able to 'float'.

An alternative method is to heat the air in the envelope. Air expands when heated and so if the air in the balloon can be heated the expansion will cause air to 'overflow'. Once the excess 200 kg of air has been expelled the balloon will be able to 'float' in the surrounding air. Although the envelope still contains the same volume of air, this air is now 'thinner' or less dense. It weighs less per cubic metre. The warmer air becomes the lower its density. If still more heat is added and more air driven from the envelope the craft becomes lighter than the air it displaces and will therefore rise.

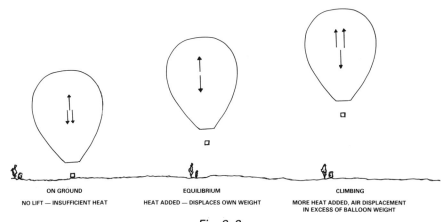

ON GROUND

NO LIFT — INSUFFICIENT HEAT

EQUILIBRIUM

HEAT ADDED — DISPLACES OWN WEIGHT

CLIMBING

MORE HEAT ADDED, AIR DISPLACEMENT
IN EXCESS OF BALLOON WEIGHT

Fig. 8–3

One disadvantage of this method is that the heat applied is continuously being dissipated to its surroundings and as the contained air cools and contracts, cold air is drawn into the envelope with a resulting loss of lift or buoyancy. As the air cools the balloon sinks.

However there is an easy way to overcome the problem. Repeated inputs of heat will keep the air in the envelope expanded and the craft buoyant. Hence the introduction of a propane burner which can control the temperature of the air inside the envelope during flight.

Balloon Volume
The greater the volume of air in an envelope the greater the amount of air displaced when heated, and therefore the greater the lifting capacity.
   In the UK volumes are quoted in thousands of cubic feet:

   i.e: size AX4 (UK 31) = 31,000 cu ft volume
        This volume of air, when heated, will displace sufficient to lift the weight of the balloon and one person.

        size AX6 (UK 56) = 56,000 cu ft volume
        This volume of hot air will generally lift the weight of the balloon plus two or possibly three persons.

Lift
There are also other factors which influence the weight a balloon can lift. Temperature and air pressure both affect the density of the air around us and therefore the weight of a specific volume of air is not a constant figure.

The **temperature** of the air outside the balloon is known as the **ambient temperature**. If the ambient temperature is high the air inside the balloon will need to be raised even higher to cause sufficient expansion and displacement. On a hot summer's day it may not be possible to raise the internal temperature sufficiently to produce the lift necessary for the balloon to fly safely, since there is a limit to the temperature balloon fabric can take.

Air pressure or barometric pressure varies all the time with the differing weather patterns. With high pressure the air becomes more dense and with low pressure the density is reduced.
   Both temperature and pressure therefore can have an effect on the actual weight of a cubic metre of air, with a resulting effect on the volume of air to be displaced from the envelope before equilibrium can be achieved.
   Temperature and pressure decrease with altitude. Assuming a constant envelope temperature, it can be taken that the drop in temperature at altitude compensates for the fall in pressure:

   i.e to maintain buoyancy;
     • as the ambient temperature decreases the internal temperature needed also decreases
     • less heat is required
     but
     • the accompanying drop in air pressure results in less dense air so more needs to be driven out
     • more heat is required

   Before any balloon flight is made the actual lifting capacity of the balloon has to be calculated to ensure that overloading does not occur, and that the balloon will have sufficient 'spare' lift to carry the proposed crew and fuel for the flight. If excess weight is carried, it may still be possible to raise the envelope temperature sufficiently for the balloon to fly, but this will be at a higher internal temperature than is safe for the balloon fabric. Standard balloons are designed to fly with a crown temperature of 100°C. Higher temperatures for any length of time will cause fabric deterioration. Obviously the higher temperatures occur in the upper part of the envelope and it is in the crown where the earliest deterioration of fabric is found.

(Thunder & Colt)

Fig. 8–6   Heated air creates lift

Load calculations are carried out using a load chart to calculate the total safe lift possible for a specific volume of balloon. It appears a rather daunting task to a new student pilot but becomes quite simple with practice.

Load chart
Based on static lift at 100°C envelope temperature.

ISA (International Standard Atmosphere) representing variation of temperature with height.

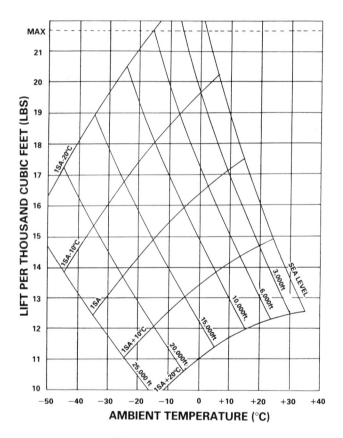

Fig. 8–4   Load chart

To find the available lift per 1000 cubic feet
— locate the relevant point on the horizontal axis indicating the ambient temperature.
— read vertically to the point where this temperature crosses the take-off flight level. (Normally taken as sea level.)
— from this point trace an ISA line, interpolating between the nearest two ISA lines drawn on the chart.

— where this line crosses the intended maximum flight altitude, read across to the vertical axis for the available lift per 1000 cubic feet.

The available lift figure is then multiplied by the relevant capacity of the balloon in thousands of feet, resulting in a **gross lift** weight in pounds:

gross lift = available lift x thousands of cu ft
i.e. multiply by 77 for a 77,000 cu ft balloon
65 for a 65,000 cu ft balloon
56 for a 56,000 cu ft balloon
31 for a 31,000 cu ft balloon

This figure gives the total lifting capacity of the balloon. Therefore, in order to arrive at the **payload**, or the additional load the empty balloon can carry (fuel, passengers, equipment etc.) the weight of the empty balloon must be taken into account:

payload = gross lift — empty weight

— the empty weight of the balloon should be stated in the balloon log-book.
— never exceed the maximum lift for your balloon size or intended maximum flight altitude.

For conversion of — pounds to kilograms multiply by: 0.4536
— kilograms to pounds multiply by: 2.2046

An **alternative method** of calculating **gross lift** using the same load chart can be done by commencing with the temperature at the intended maximum altitude of a flight. If the temperature at this altitude has not been given in a pre-flight met. forecast it can be estimated by subtracting two degrees for every thousand feet of altitude from the ambient temperature at the launch site:

— locate the relevant point on the horizontal axis indicating this temperature.
— read vertically to the point where this temperature crosses the maximum altitude level.
— from this point read across the vertical axis for the available lift per 1000 cubic feet.

The **payload calculation remains the same**:

payload = gross lift − empty weight

An **inversion** requires a slightly different approach to the calculations. In this case the temperature rises with increased height and a payload calculated on cooler ground temperatures could lead to overloading. It is better to use temperatures predicted for mid-day or alternatively to leave a decent margin below the maximum calculated weight.

Example

To calculate the payload for a 77,000 cu ft balloon:

- empty weight   400 lb   or 181.4 kg
- ambient temperature   +20°C
- maximum altitude   10,000 ft

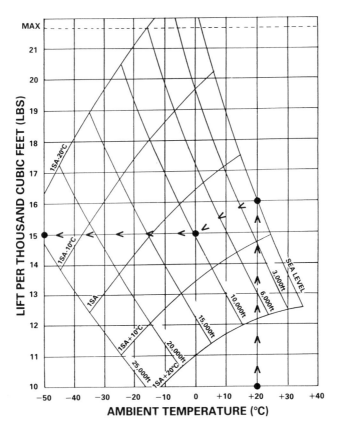

Fig. 8–5   Load chart – see example calculation

By following the broken line on the chart a figure of 15 lb (6.8 kg) lift per 1000 feet is arrived at.

gross lift = available lift x thousands of cu ft

Gross lift = 15 x 77 = 1155 lb   **or**   Gross lift = 6.8 x 77 = 523.9 kg

payload = gross lift — empty weight

Payload = 1155 − 400 = 755 lb   **or**   Payload = 523.9 − 181.4 = 342.5 kg

Loading

	755 lb	342.5 kg
Less 3 flight cylinders @ 70 lb/32 kg each	210	96
	545 lb	246.5 kg
Less equipment (helmets, maps, camera etc.)	10	4.5
	535 lb	242 kg
Less pilot @ 150 lb/68 kg	150	68
Balance left for remaining crew	385 lb	174 kg

It will be seen from this example that there is enough 'spare lift' to carry two crew if they do not weigh a lot more than the pilot.

A pilot who regularly flies the same balloon, can save a little time in calculating spare lift by adding his weight, together with those of the full flight cylinders and other equipment normally carried, to the empty weight of the balloon. This figure can then be used before each flight to produce the spare lift available for crew or passengers, without the need for further calculations.

SECTION 2

FLIGHT TRAINING

9

FLIGHT PREPARATION

Weather Conditions
Careful consideration of the existing and forecast weather conditions for any planned flight of the balloon is of vital importance. The overall weather pattern; including surface and upper wind speeds and direction, temperatures, visibility and cloud conditions; all must be studied — both actual and forecast for the duration of planned flight and beyond.

Keeping an eye on TV weather bulletins is a good way of spotting the possibility of good ballooning conditions to come, but these forecasts are of a very general nature and usually more information is required.

A pre-recorded low level aviation forecast, **AIRMET**, is available by telephone. There are three AIRMET regions, Scottish, Northern and Southern (England). Each region is subdivided into numbered areas. The forecast is given in a standard form which can be transcribed on to a Pilot's Proforma. (Copies of this are obtainable, free of charge, on receipt of SAE — A4 size — from AOPA or Airtour International.) This forecast can be supplemented on request by a forecast office if at least two hours notice is given.

Another helpful meteorological service is **VOLMET**: frequently updated information from various airfields broadcast on VHF airband radio.

It is also possible to subscribe to a specialist forecasting system which is charged per report plus the cost of the telephone call to the forecasting office, and Prestel carries an aviation met. report too.

Because as balloonists we require such a specific met. report for a very localised area it is often impossible to get as much information as we would like. A windspeed of five knots five miles down the road can exist alongside a windspeed of 10–15 knots at the launch site. Also, even after the most detailed reports have been received the actual weather can be quite different at take-off, only thirty minutes or so later.

A helium-filled balloon released at the launch site is probably the best indication of the actual wind direction at launch time and a guide to local turbulence.

Surface winds in excess of fifteen knots are not considered suitable for launching and indeed inexperienced pilots would be well advised to accept a much lower figure as an upper limit, i.e. 8–10 knots. Wind direction is of course relative to the area being flown. **Downwind hazards** may be the deciding factor i.e. coastal regions/airspace restrictions/built-up areas, etc.

Thermic activity and cumulus cloud build ups are both causes and indications of **instability** which make balloon flying inadvisable. The craft becomes very unstable and unpredictable as far as controllability is concerned in these conditions.

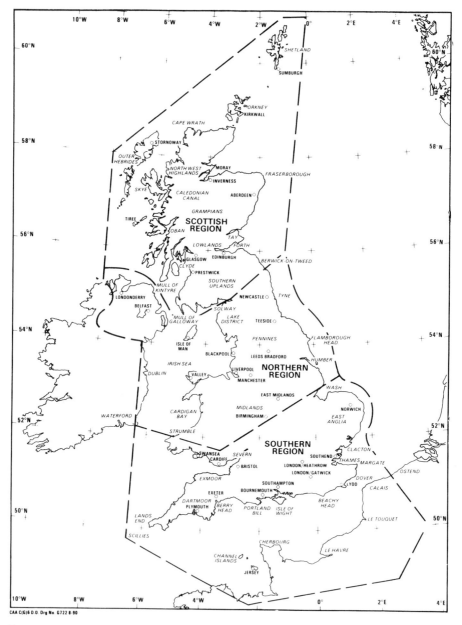

CAA C(G)6 D.O. Drg No. G722 8-90

The name places shown on the map will be used by forecasters to locate the position of fronts and other weather features.

Fig. 9–0   Airmet boundaries and regions

If flight is considered beneath a cloud layer, there must be ample clearance between any high ground or built-up area and cloud, to allow safe and legal flight (VMC) between the two.

The **temperature** to be encountered, both on the ground and in the air, is another factor to be taken into consideration. This will affect the loading of the balloon. (See Chapter 8 for load chart and calculations.)

Flight in **rain** is not advisable. Visibility is severely reduced and the added weight of water on the fabric makes flying extremely difficult. A lot of this water will also find its way down on to the occupants of the basket to add to their discomfort! Pilot lights do not take kindly either to being dowsed with water.

Choice of site

Never use any site for launching the balloon without the **permission** of the landowner, occupier or controller. Even with permission, check that there are no animals on adjacent properties which could take fright.

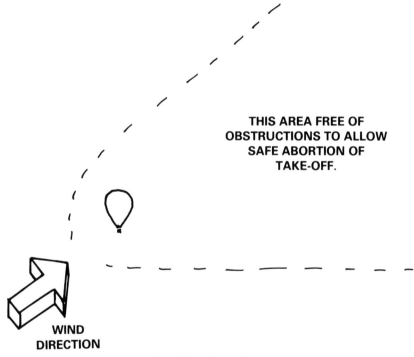

THIS AREA FREE OF OBSTRUCTIONS TO ALLOW SAFE ABORTION OF TAKE-OFF.

WIND DIRECTION

Fig. 9–1   Launch area

Shelter is desirable on a launch site where surface windspeeds are above 3–5 knots. This needs to be in some form of wind shadow, i.e. a good bank of trees, or a low lying area with some sort of cover to break the wind. Buildings are a poor choice usually because the wind merely comes round the sides and over the top and aims at the downwind side with a resulting increase in turbulence.

The site should also have an **unobstructed down wind area** to allow for an aborted take-off, for whatever reason. This area needs to be in the form of a fan shape leading out from the launch point to something in the order of 150–200 yards depending on windspeed. The higher the windspeed the longer and wider the area needs to be. The surface should not be one that is likely to damage the fabric of the balloon.

Check there are no dangerous downwind obstacles i.e power lines, or very tall trees. Also ensure that the surface is not likely to cause damage to the envelope. Car parks or similar surfaces can be very damaging to an envelope as small stones or gravel can easily penetrate the ripstop fabric if the envelope drags on inflation or is trodden on by over enthusiastic crew.

The site should have good **access** for vehicles. Following wet weather, ensure that the vehicle can be driven without bogging down in long grass or muddy gateways.

Also check that the launch site is not situated within controlled airspace.

Loading
Using a load chart calculate the payload you can carry on the flight. Decide on the number of fuel cylinders and passengers the balloon can lift. See Chapter 8 for an explanation of the load chart.

Flight path
The OS map and 1:500,000 air chart should be studied along the expected track of flight to familiarise oneself with sensitive areas, recognisable navigational features and air information. It helps to transfer air information onto the OS 1:50,000 map to be used. An Airtour Balloon Calculator can make this task a lot easier and quicker.

Crew briefing
The pilot is responsible for briefing all crew members to ensure that everyone knows their own role during inflation and take-off. The main theme must be safety with special emphasis on the point that no-one should allow themselves to be lifted off the ground. (See Chapter 7: Crew and Crew Briefing.)

Passenger briefing
Passengers must be fully aware of what to expect on a flight. They must appreciate that the pilot is in charge and that they must be prepared to carry out any orders from him. It is most important that they know where not to hold, i.e. the fuel lines or rip line should not be used as hand-holds. The whereabouts of the internal rope handles should be clearly pointed out so passengers know exactly where they can take a firm hold during landing.

Instruct passengers to have knees slightly bent on landing to help absorb the impact and avoid the chance of spinal or other injuries. It is better not to face forward but rather to be backwards or sideways on to the direction of landing. Holding on in two separate places is steadier than having both hands on the same hand-hold. It must be stressed that arms and hands must be kept within the basket when landing. Anything outside at this time stands a chance of being caught under the basket rim with the likelihood once more of serious injuries. It must be stressed that no-one may leave the basket without the pilot's permission — at any time.

As with every one involved with the balloon, the passengers should know that smoking is not allowed in or around the basket and propane cylinders. A majority of passengers will wish to carry their cameras with them. Make sure that cameras can be stowed safely for landing.

When meeting passengers for the first time it is in the pilot's interest to ascertain that they are physically fit. No-one wants to be in the situation where a passenger collapses miles from anywhere during a long carry out.

A simple information list handed to a new passenger can be very helpful in ensuring that they are fully aware of what is expected of them.

GENERAL BRIEFING FOR BALLOON PASSENGERS

TO FLY OR NOT TO FLY IS ENTIRELY THE INDIVIDUAL PILOT'S DECISION.

THE PILOT OF THE BALLOON RESERVES THE RIGHT TO REFUSE TO FLY ANY PASSENGER.

SMOKING IS NOT ALLOWED ON BOARD OR IN THE VICINITY OF THE BALLOON.

COMPLIANCE WITH ANY ORDER FROM THE BALLOON PILOT IS ESSENTIAL.

★　　★　　★　　★　　★

Protective headgear should be available and worn if requested by the pilot.

ON TAKE-OFF
When the pilot is ready you will be asked to enter the basket. Do not hold on to any fuel lines, control lines or the red rip line when doing so.

Once in the basket there will be rope handles to hold on to just below the rim. (One or possibly two on each side.) Stand where the pilot indicates and do not move around the basket unless asked to do so.

AT NO TIME LEAVE THE BALLOON BASKET WITHOUT PERMISSION.

Generally there will be no sensation of lifting on take-off, the ground merely drops away.

ON LANDING
The pilot will advise you where to stand in the basket when he is preparing to land. Ensure all camera equipment etc. is safely stowed.

Knees should be slightly bent on landing to absorb any impact without injury.

Hold only on to the rope handles WITHIN THE BASKET and avoid holding on to fuel lines, control lines or rip line.

DO NOT HOLD ON TO THE TOP RIM OF THE BASKET.

Even when the balloon appears stationary after landing, do not leave the basket until given permission to do so by the pilot.

PHYSICAL FITNESS
If you suffer from any of the following please bring them to the attention of the pilot: epilepsy, fits, giddiness, blackouts, heart disease, spinal problems, diabetes, recent surgery, any physical disability.

From ARTICLE 53 of the Air Navigation Order
  'A person must not board any aircraft when drunk or be drunk in it . . .'

10

EQUIPMENT AND CONTROLS

This book is not intended as a substitute for the balloon manufacturer's handbook which should always be consulted for any query on an individual balloon.

A pilot should be aware of and stay within the manufacturer's operational limitations, not only in the interests of safety but also since operation outside these limits will invalidate a C of A.

Unloading equipment

Everyone packs their balloon in the most convenient manner for their particular vehicle, so unloading is just a matter of the logical removal of it all, taking care not to damage anything. It is advisable to lift heavy items with assistance. Care must be taken when lifting fuel tanks, where rough handling could damage an internal dip-tube. Covers and straps which are removed before rigging the balloon should be stowed in convenient places where crew can find them when packing away after the flight. It saves time and effort when doing this if the pilot can indicate exactly where he wants things placed. Wind direction has to be decided so that the basket can be placed in the upwind position with the envelope ready to be pulled out in the downwind direction.

Rigging basket/burner assembly

With the basket upright load in the fuel cylinders. Each pilot light on the burner system will need to be fed from a master fuel cylinder with a vapour take-off outlet, other cylinders carried can be slave cylinders which only have a liquid take-off. The cylinders should be secured in the basket using two straps per cylinder. Two cylinders should be orientated so that one will supply vapour to the pilot light to be used for inflation and the other, liquid propane to the main burner, when the basket is on its side for inflation. Tanks are labelled to indicate which way they need to be to supply vapour or liquid.

The burner then needs to be fitted above the basket by means of the nylon support poles. Some pilots prefer to locate the poles in the basket sockets and lift the burner up on to poles to align them with the burner frame sockets, others locate the poles in the burner frame and then lift the whole assembly on to the basket to line up with those sockets. The basket wires are connected to the burner frame by means of carabiners at four location points, and the protective covers fitted around the support poles and basket wires. Most pilots also enclose the fuel hoses in these covers.

Now everything is ready for the burner system to be tested. When testing the burner it is important to avoid the danger of a possible propane leak catching fire. Therefore the pilot light is not lit until the part of the

Fig. 10–1   Fully rigged balloon

system under test has been connected and no sign of leaking detected. It is a procedure that with practice becomes a good habit, although it can appear rather complicated to the new student pilot. Gloves should always be worn when handling the burner or propane.

Burner test
- check all tank valves are in the 'off' position
- check all burner valves are in the 'off' position
- connect hoses to appropriate cylinders
- open one liquid feed valve on cylinder
- check for leaks — listen, look and sniff (hissing, frosting on joints, smell of propane)
- open one vapour feed valve on cylinder
- check for leaks
- light pilot light (having opened burner pilot light valve if fitted)
- open main burner valve — check flame appears normal
                              — check operating burner pressure (some gauges register pressure in hose before burner valve is opened)
- close main burner valve
- close liquid feed valve on cylinder
- open main burner valve again to burn off liquid propane in hose
- 'pop' pilot light hose, close pilot light valves on burner and cylinder
- repeat above for all remaining hoses and cylinders

NB. The silent burner should be tested when there is liquid propane in the hose on its feed side.

Ensure that the operational pressure of the burner is above the minimum recommended in the manufacturer's handbook. If not, it may be possible to increase the flight cylinder pressure. (See Chapter 26 — Propane Handling.)

In the interests of safety it is advisable to vent lines by burning off the propane rather than releasing liquid propane.

It is worth bearing in mind at this point that, when the inflation commences, everything practical should have been done in preparation for actual flight, even if a free flight is not intended. Then if the balloon breaks free as a result of some emergency or failure on the ground, the pilot can safely opt to make a flight.

Therefore, before the basket is tipped on to its side, check that the instrument pack is installed and that batteries do not need replacing. All maps needed for the flight should be stowed ready for use and the fire extinguisher should be in a position that makes it easily accessible not only when the basket is upright but also when on its side for inflation.

When tipping the basket over, do not support the weight by the burner or nylon poles.

Rigging envelope
The envelope bag should be placed about ten feet in front of the burner assembly, the flying wires withdrawn and orientated in their correct sequence. The mouth of the envelope will have some indication as to which is centre top or centre bottom for inflation, which will also help with sorting out the layout of the wires. The flying wires are divided between the four connection points (i.e. three wires per carabiner for a twelve gore, two wires for an eight gore). Each set connects to the load frame either into a basket wire carabiner or a separate one, taking care that there are no twisted or crossed wires.

When all four sets of wires are connected up and the carabiner screw-gates closed the bag may be carried away downwind, allowing the envelope to spill out and finally unroll at the crown end; the crown line being taken away further downwind until it is lying completely unravelled, in line with the envelope and basket.

At this stage some balloonists prefer to spread out the envelope on the ground so that the underside is completely flat to enable the cold inflation to take place quickly and easily. Others prefer to start the inflation fan straight away and let the force of the cold air untwist and unfold the fabric. One simple way to spread out the envelope is for two people to work opposite one another, pulling out on the load tape which leads up from the uppermost flying wire of the bottom set on each side. Care should be taken to only hold on to load tapes and not to pull or stand on the fabric, which could cause damage.

Before any air is introduced to the envelope the quick release restraint must be connected to the burner frame and vehicle. This is a short line (five metres or less) to prevent the balloon becoming airborne before the pilot is ready. It should not be attached to the rear of a trailer since this could be lifted off the ground by the pull of the balloon. It is not a tether line but one which is released by the pilot from the basket when he is ready to lift-off. For this reason there has to be some method of releasing the line in one quick operation. Several types of quick release fittings are available, or the pilot may prefer to tie a quick release knot. Use of a quick release restraint is now mandatory for training flights and checkouts.

All pilots should be aware of the BBAC's Safety Code. (See Chapter 24.)

11

INFLATION TECHNIQUES

Cold Inflation
The pilot should check that all connections are correctly made and that the quick release is in position before starting the inflation fan and introducing cold air into the envelope. One or two crew will be needed to hold open the mouth of the balloon. If it has not already been done, brief the crew and passengers (see Chapter 7) before the inflation fan is started as it is difficult to converse over the noise it makes. This is also a good moment to ensure that spectators are safely behind the basket. Where there is a large crowd, one crew member should be delegated to crowd control. Warn people of the loudness of the burner, especially those with young children and dogs. In certain circumstances it may be necessary to rope off the launch area in accordance with minimum clearances laid down by the CAA.

Until the envelope is in an upright position the parachute will not have sufficient pressure behind it to stay in place. Therefore it will need to be secured in position to prevent cold air being lost from the top of the envelope. There will be Velcro tabs on the parachute and also round the top rim of the envelope. Usually these will be numbered to ensure correct orientation of the parachute. Corresponding tabs should be pressed together taking care that no cords or load tapes are caught up between tabs.

When there is sufficient air in the envelope to enable a clear view of the rigging points the pilot should commence his walk round inspection inside. There is no substitute for this although some pilots are reluctant to walk inside their envelope for fear of causing damage. However, close inspection of sewn attachment points cannot be made by peering in from the mouth or top and a walk-in inspection is certainly recommended on a regular basis, if not before every flight. Starting at the rip line location point, inspect the stitching of the attachment loop and the knot securing the line and then follow the rip line up to the parachute pulley. This should be checked for free running, especially following any repairs to the envelope, when loose threads can become caught up and cause jamming. A jammed pulley can lead to friction on the rip line, melting the rope and making it brittle. By running the line through the fingers as you walk along such changes can be detected.

While standing at the parachute pulley the parachute lines can be checked to see that they are free from tangles and properly secured at the attachment locations on both the envelope and the parachute. Still following the rip line the rip pulley and attachment point can be inspected and then the rope/wire junction if the line is not a continuous kevlar one. Finally the line's attachment to the burner frame is checked. The line

Fig. 11–1   Walk in checks

usually has a spring clip or small carabiner at this end which hooks into a carabiner on the load frame or into a special location point for the rip line.

A check should also be made to ensure that the temperature streamer is still in position, and the heat sensitive label should be checked for signs of overheating from the previous flight.

There are a small number of balloon envelopes which do not have a parachute venting system. Instead they have Velcro holding together one of the circular seams in the crown around two thirds of the circumference. When the rip line is operated the Velcro is pulled apart, opening up the crown and releasing the air from the envelope. This Velcro has to be closed and inspected before cold inflation takes place. It is a job which requires three people. Two hold adjacent vertical tape junctions across a gore, keeping a steady tension on the Velcro, and the third closes the Velcro in the correct alignment, firmly pressing the surfaces together. To avoid accidental opening of the Velcro in flight there are points which are fitted with 'rip-locks' which need to be fastened as well. Some also require 'tying off' with thread as an extra precaution. A positive tug on the rip line releases these when needed.

Hot Inflation
Once everything has been checked and the crew is in position the pilot should be ready to start the hot inflation which will lift the envelope off the ground and into the upright position. The crew should all be informed that the pilot is ready to commence, either verbally or in the case of the person on the crown line by a pre-arranged signal. Any spectators should also be asked to step back behind the basket line and to keep safely out of the way during the inflation operation.

It pays to be patient at this point and let the inflation fan fill the envelope with as much cold air as possible. In good conditions the envelope can fill sufficiently to dispense with the need for crew to hold open the mouth and when the burner is turned on the hot air fills the envelope in a far more controlled manner making the job of letting the crown up much less work too.

It is important for a pilot to realise that when the burner is on it is virtually impossible to communicate other than by hand signals. He must keep half an eye on the crew whilst inflating in case they need to attract his attention.

A pilot must not leave the burner unattended once inflation has commenced. To start inflation the pilot light needs to be ignited — the cylinder valve to one vapour feed is opened, followed by the pilot valve on the burner. The vapour is then ignited either by external means, or by the built-in ignitor on the burner itself. Even when using a burner fitted with more than one pilot light, inflation is never done with more than one primed or lit. This is in the interests of safety on the ground. Should there be a leak or fire at this point the less fuel already in fuel lines the better. It is obviously speedier to shut down one rather than two pilot flames in an

(Arthur Williams)

Fig. 11–2   Hot inflation

emergency, and there is only one flame to ignite any leak should one occur. Only one cylinder liquid valve is then opened for the same reasons and the pilot is ready to open the main burner. Before doing so he should inform crew and spectators — usually by shouting 'burning!'

The inflation fan should be kept running during the application of heat until the envelope is clear of the ground and the fan no longer blowing air into it. Care should be taken in directing the fan so that the burner flame is not blown sideways towards crew at the mouth. If the fan is switched off too early the sides of the mouth tend to suck in, increasing the chance of fabric scorching. When the fan is no longer an advantage the pilot should indicate for it to be turned off. It should also be moved quickly away if at all possible to prevent it being damaged by the basket as it lifts upright or becoming tangled in the flying wires.

In good conditions the envelope can be inflated relatively quickly using long burns with very short pauses to ensure that crew etc. are all right. Short bursts of heat in these conditions often cause the envelope to lose the pressure it had with the cold air and the sides pull in distorting the mouth while the envelope is still on the ground. The inflation consequently takes a lot longer and is more difficult for the crew to control.

However, in gusty conditions it is difficult to keep the envelope still and pressurised with cold air and the heat has to be introduced using short bursts on the burner to avoid damage to the mouth of the balloon. The inflation fan may have to be abandoned early if the envelope is moving too much and in danger of knocking the fan over. In such conditions it is sensible to have one person with the sole responsibility of controlling the fan as directed.

Once the envelope and basket start to lift spare crew can apply their weight to the basket to keep it on the ground and as soon as the outfit is upright the mouth crew can also transfer their weight to the basket. If the envelope is fitted with a scoop the clips should be attached to the burner frame. At this point the crown line crew may still be trying to hold down an upright crown — so the pilot should signal for the line to be brought in and attached to the basket. There are several methods of securing this line, either to the burner frame or the upright support poles. Whatever method is used it should be one which is easy to release. If the envelope has an encounter with trees at some point in the flight the line is quite likely to become tangled in branches and needs to be able to pull free if the balloon is to continue in the air. Large loops, toggles or clips on the end which could jam in between branches are not to be recommended either.

With the balloon upright, the pilot then puts in enough heat to stabilise it prior to working through the pre-flight checks.

12

THE TAKE-OFF

Pre-flight checks
Many pilots have difficulty in remembering the check list until experience makes it a routine habit. Everyone has their own order of checking through the list but one way to remember things initially is to go through the following mnemonic one letter at a time:–

'T I M E   F O R   L I F T'

Tabs
The Velcro tabs which held the parachute in place during the inflation now need to be broken apart to enable the parachute to seal correctly. Heat is put into the envelope and the pilot warns the crew to hold the basket down firmly. The rip line is pulled sharply until the seals are broken and is then quickly released to avoid unnecessary loss of heat. As the parachute reseals the envelope will 'bounce' which could lift the basket if it is not held down by crew.

Instruments
The altimeter must be set to allow for the daily changes in pressure. Setting the height to the field elevation of the take-off site can be done if height is known. (OS Maps will show this.) Alternatively the pressure can be set to the regional QNH. Check that the variometer is switched on and the thermister connected if one is installed. Switch on radio.

Maps
Ensure that sufficient maps are carried to cover not only the indicated flight path but with allowance for deviation and for extended flight. Windspeed and direction can vary considerably during the course of some flights. A 1:500,000 air chart should also be carried, and although not mandatory, a 1:250,000 chart could be useful should a flight extend beyond the OS maps on board for any reason.

Extinguisher
Check to see that the fire extinguisher is in a readily accessible position, especially if it has been placed elsewhere to be convenient during inflation.

Fuel
The second fuel system should now be turned on at the cylinder to be ready for use. Ensure that there is sufficient fuel carried for the intended duration of flight plus an ample reserve.

Obstacles
The downwind obstacles, if any, need to be noted and taking into account the current windspeed the rate at which the balloon has to climb out can be assessed.

Retrieve
Where no radio communication is carried it is important that the pilot and ground crew have agreed on a common telephone number they can use to leave messages should they lose contact with each other. A quick check that the pilot does not have the car keys in his pocket can save a lot of hassle later on too.

Lines, wires and carabiners
The internal rigging lines should be inspected, especially the parachute lines. They should be free with no tangles or knots. The rip line needs to attached to the load frame and the free hanging portion must not be looped through any flying wires. Any other lines, i.e. rotation vent lines must also have a free run to their attachment points. The flying wires must not be crossed and all the carabiners must have their screw gates fully closed.

Ignitor
Always back up the ignition system. If there is an integral ignitor on the burner still carry an additonal means of relighting a pilot light. Whatever is carried ensure that it is readily to hand, either in the basket or a pocket. If the burner does not have its own system it is sensible to carry two different types of ignition. i.e. ignitor and matches (safety variety).

Folks
Ask the passenger(s) to embark, again emphasising where and where not to hold on to. They will then have a moment or two to settle themselves before lift-off.

Take off quick release
The pilot must now apply enough heat to the envelope to make it buoyant and ready to lift out. (If the fuel cylinder used for the inflation is not to be carried on the flight it should be closed down at this point, the hose cleared and disconnected and reconnected to a flight cylinder. The cylinder valve should then be opened, checked for leaks and the burner tested on this tank.) To check if the balloon is light the crew holding on the

(Arthur Williams)

Fig. 12–1   Lift-off

basket are instructed to raise their hands a few inches above the rim —
'Hands off'. The pilot can instantly see the state of lift and should quickly
order the crew to retain their hold by 'Hands on'. When the pilot is ready
for take-off the order 'Hands off' is given again and the quick release freed.

The rate of ascent needed is dependent on the prevailing weather
conditions and the downwind terrain. In good conditions and a clear

launch direction a gentle lift off is a more controlled procedure. In higher windspeeds or with tall obstacles to clear the balloon needs more heat so that the climb out rate is faster. This is a less controlled procedure and care should be taken not to exceed the maximum climb rate stated in the balloon's handbook. The initial climb out should be to a minimum height of 500 ft to avoid upsetting animals downwind of the launch site, which a pilot may not be aware of.

A considerate pilot remembers to thank the ground crew as he takes off. It is important to record the take-off time for pilot and balloon logbooks.

13

CLIMBING & DESCENDING

Vertical movement relative to the ground is controlled by use of the burner and parachute vent. An increase in temperature will arrest a descent, initiate or continue a climb. Use of the parachute vent will arrest a climb or initiate or increase a descent.

Often one of the most difficult things for a student pilot to assess is whether the balloon is ascending or descending. This is something which comes with experience. It is not something which can be judged by looking to the front, where the forward speed can give a misleading feeling of climbing or descending. It is best to look to one side and fixing your sights on something fairly obvious, watch how it moves in relation to another object and apply the rules of parallax.

E.g. Watching a chimney behind a large tree . . .

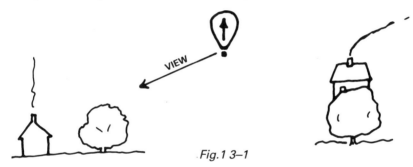

Fig.1 3–1

When climbing — the whole cottage appears.

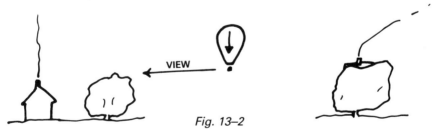

Fig. 13–2

When descending — the chimney will disappear.

With a large volume of air to heat it follows that there will be a certain delay in the action expected after applying heat to the envelope. This has to be allowed for at all times, and will take quite a bit of practice to perfect.

Climbing

To make the balloon climb the internal temperature of the envelope needs to be increased. Heat is best added using short frequent burns rather than one long one which can easily cause overheating of the fabric. To continue a climb it is simply a case of maintaining the increase in temperature. In a fast climb care should be taken not to exceed the maximum rate of climb for the balloon. (This will be found in the Operation Limitations of the manufacturer's handbook.)

Because of the delay between adding heat and the corresponding response it will take a bit of practice to get the balloon to level out at the height required. The rate of climb therefore needs to be reduced before this height is reached.

Slowing down a rate of climb is achieved by lowering the internal temperature of the envelope. Shorter burns or longer intervals between, ceasing to burn altogether or opening the parachute vent for a few seconds will all achieve this, and the method chosen depends on the rate of climb and the speed at which the climb needs arresting.

Descending

Cooling the balloon will start a descent. A gentle descent can be started by letting the envelope cool naturally; either by ceasing to apply heat altogether or simply allowing more time between burns or shortening the length of burns. A gentle descent is more controllable in that it will be easier and quicker to arrest.

A speedy descent can be initiated by letting some of the hot air out through the parachute vent. This enables much cooler air from outside to be drawn into the envelope at the mouth. It is not necessary to hold the parachute open for more than a few seconds. If no heat is applied the rate of descent will accelerate until the balloon reaches its 'cold descent rate'. At this point the envelope is still deployed but the air inside is virtually at ambient temperature — orientation can become difficult because the balloon will start rotating.

When cold descents are being practised care should be taken to reduce the rate of descent to the recommendation of the BBAC Safety Code, in that a pilot should not exceed a descent of 500 ft per minute below 500 ft agl. (See Chapter 25, General Safety.)

A student must be aware that over-use of the parachute vent, i.e. holding it open for more than a few seconds could cause too much air to escape. The air going out can cause the mouth to close up restricting the entry of cold air — there is not enough pressure inside to close the parachute vent even if it is released and the envelope may lose its shape and 'candle'. Turning on the burner will have little effect other than to set alight the closed mouth. It is therefore safer to release a small amount of air in the first instance and repeat the operation if this is not sufficient.

To arrest a descent, short bursts of heat should be used at frequent intervals to build up the temperature again until the descent is halted. Using long bursts of heat can endanger the fabric.

Encountering windshear

Sometimes a sudden change of windspeed or direction is met when ascending or descending. This is known as windshear. When the envelope enters a different flow of air it attempts to follow it and can often receive quite a buffeting in the process. This can result in loss of lift through loss of air and this needs to be replaced by getting heat into the envelope fairly rapidly. The buffeting may distort the envelope dramatically so care must be taken not to burn the mouth area whilst replenishing the heat. Less dramatic windshear effects can be a feeling of wind in the face — when the balloon is entering a slower airstream; or a feeling of wind from behind when the balloon is accelerating into a faster moving airstream; or simply a change of direction.

14

STRAIGHT & LEVEL FLIGHT

In the flight test a student has to demonstrate straight and level flight for a minimum of five minutes.

The aim of the exercise is to keep the temperature of the envelope constant at the balloon's level of equilibrium. This is best done by short frequent bursts of heat which give a resulting flight path like a very gentle sine wave.

Fig. 14–1   Shallow sine wave

The novice will find this harder than it sounds, especially if there are problems in sensing whether the balloon is ascending or descending. Initially the rate of burning is usually overdone, and so longer pauses are needed to compensate for this. If burns are too far apart the envelope will have cooled more each time and a longer burn will be needed to bring the temperature back up. The flight path here will be a far more pronounced sine wave or 'yo-yo'.

Fig. 14–2   Deep sine wave

Practice is the only way to become proficient at level flying. Again, look to one side to determine whether the balloon is ascending or descending. Eventually this will become an almost reflex action and the judgement of where on the sine curve to burn, to keep it shallow, will become easier. A variometer or a rate of climb or descent indicator may indicate level flight, but there could be a lag on the readings, and so a student should not become reliant on these instruments. Often an instructor will stand in front of the instrument pack to make a student think for him/herself. It is easier at low level to judge what the balloon is doing but this can only be practised over suitable terrain.

15

IN-FLIGHT NAVIGATION

Map reading to the new student can seem an almost impossible task to perform whilst also concentrating on keeping the balloon airborne. However it is important that a pilot knows his position at all times. Firstly so that no infringements are made into controlled airspace without permission, secondly that landowner sensitive areas are overflown at suitable heights and thirdly that the exact landing position is known.

By law a 1:500,000 ICAO chart has to be carried to cover the area flown but using it for navigation would be very difficult because of the small scale. The speed at which a balloon flies is so slow in relation to other aircraft that even the 1:250,000 air chart used by most PPL's is still scaled down too much for balloon navigation. However this is a handy chart to carry in case the flight unexpectedly extends beyond the area covered by the larger scale maps on board. This chart shows aeronautical information in good detail, but only up to 3000 ft — a factor to bear in mind if flight higher than 3000 ft is intended.

For most flying the best charts to use are the Ordnance Survey, 1:50,000 scale which show features in good detail, making for easy flight orientation. Because these are large scale maps several may be needed to adequately cover the area to be flown. (Allowances have to be made for unexpected changes in wind direction.)

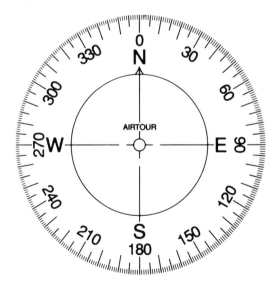

Fig. 15–1   Compass rose

Because a map is a rather cumbersome sheet of paper to have to handle in the confines of the balloon basket many pilots prefer to fold the one in use around a map board. The launch area should be clearly marked so it can be picked out easily. If it is a regularly used site it can help to stick a transparent compass rose over it which will help in ascertaining direction of flight on lift off, and also with pre-flight planning using the forecast wind direction.

Unfortunately, a normal flight path does not follow a straight line, otherwise it would be a simple matter of drawing a line at lift-off in the direction taken and picking out features along this to pinpoint your location. Therefore the map will need marking at regular intervals to show the balloon's location and track. Some people like a permanent record of every flight done and mark on their maps with a pen. However this can become confusing if a lot of flying is done in the same area. Marking with pencil which can easily be erased is probably a better method. If the maps are covered with transparent plastic they can be drawn on in chinagraph pencil, which can be wiped off. Crosses or dots should be made on the map, either at regular intervals or when crossing an easily recognisable landmark. If preferred these marks can be joined to mark the track more clearly. It is also helpful to jot down the time occasionally to assist with calculating speed or fuel consumption. An important consideration is that the map is not viewed continuously and therefore the last marked position needs to be easily picked out when the map is looked at again.

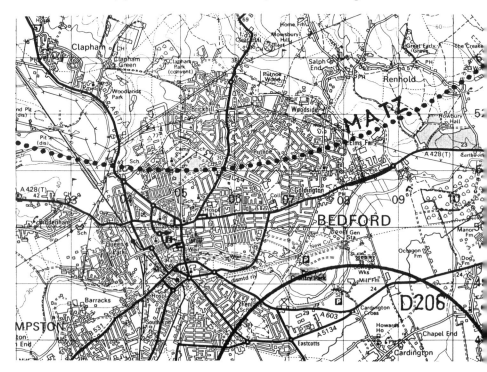

Fig. 15–2   Marking track on map: note boundaries of MATZ and danger area

Study the map before take-off. To familiarise oneself with obvious features along the anticipated flight path can save a lot of time when trying to map-read once airborne. A light pencil line ruled in the anticipated direction of flight can sometimes be a help with initial orientation.

Recording the track on the map is helpful for more than just knowing your exact location at any time. Using an Airtour Ballooning calculator your flight speed can be calculated between two points, and this in turn can help with other calculations.

For example: there may be a large built-up area ahead. Using your speed you can estimate the time it will take to reach/overfly the area. You can then estimate whether you have sufficient fuel on board (which must include an ample safety reserve) to fly beyond this area, or whether you must land before reaching it.

Another way of judging speed is to mark the track on the map at six minute intervals — some watches can be set to give an alarm at regular intervals — this spacing being one tenth of an hour means that the speed is 10 x distance covered (in knots, miles per hour or kilometres per hour, depending on how distance is recorded).

Measurement in	nautical miles	= speed in knots
	statute miles	= speed in miles per hour
	kilometres	= speed in kilometres per hour

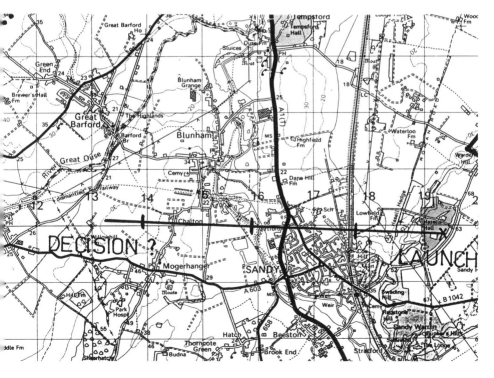

It may be noticed that different heights show movement in differing directions and speeds. These can be used to gain some degree of steering, especially in competition flying.

It is always worth noting the direction of the ground wind since it will be a factor to consider when planning for a landing. There are usually chimneys smoking or bonfires going which will show this direction for you.

If the regular markings on the map begin to appear further and further apart, this is an indication that the windspeed has picked up. If the speed increases significantly just watching the ground passing by below will be a clear indication of this. At low level it is often possible to hear the rustle of the wind in the trees or fields of standing corn as they are passed over.

Other factors can affect the direction of flight at low level. Ground features such as valleys or hills can play their part in changes of flight direction. A valley running across the direction of travel will have an air current flowing along to the left or right and likewise the wind will be directed around one side or the other of a steep hill. Such features can be picked out on the map by examining the contour lines. Lines close together indicate a steep slope. The numbering of the contours will clarify whether you are looking at an uphill or downhill slope.

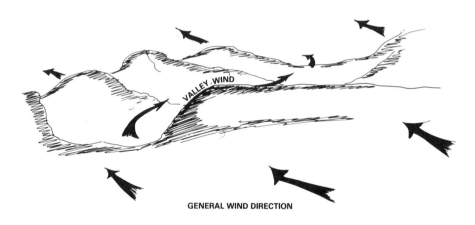

GENERAL WIND DIRECTION

Fig. 15–3   Valley wind currents

If for any reason you cannot locate your position on the map it is important to make every effort to find it. This is not always easy to do at very low level, but a climb to show more of the countryside will give the chance to pick out more landmarks. Pick some very clear feature visible on the ground and attempt to pick it out on the map, or vice versa. By then plotting your bearing from this marker on the map, it should be possible to pick out a closer landmark along this line to pinpoint your exact position. Alternatively select two good features and by plotting your bearing from each you should be able to discover your whereabouts.

(If totally lost and carrying radio, perhaps retrieve can give you a clue to your location!)

Potential hazards to balloons such as power lines and tall aerials etc. will have been picked out on the map before flight but it should be noted that not all power lines are shown. On seeing wires which do not appear on your map, do not panic and imagine yourself lost — check your location with other features first!

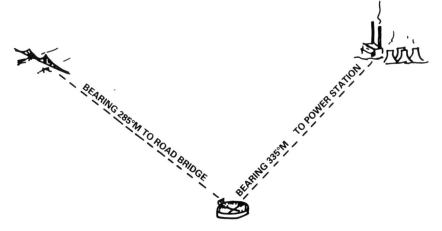

Fig. 15–4   Finding bearings

16

EMERGENCY SITUATIONS & PROCEDURES

An **emergency** is defined as an unexpected happening of a dangerous or worrying nature, requiring very quick action. In flight emergencies can be classed as major or minor. A major emergency may not be resolved and will require the balloon to make an emergency landing, while a minor one can usually be rectified to some degree and therefore time can be taken to select a safe convenient site for a precautionary landing.

Emergency landing
Any emergency arising during the flight which is not resolved at once will call for an 'emergency landing'. That is to say a landing that is made as quickly as possible — the priority being to get all occupants quickly and safely back on the ground. In such a situation it may not be possible to avoid damage to the balloon.

If the balloon is not descending initiate one by opening the parachute for short periods of roughly five seconds a time.

Instruct passengers to put on and fasten crash helmets. Position them to the front of the basket, holding on tightly to basket handles, with knees slightly bent to absorb impact. Repeat the warning not to leave the basket until asked to do so and stress that they must do whatever you ask, at once. Also give warning that the landing may be a hard or heavy one.

It is imperative to clear the fuel lines before landing so these must be closed at the cylinder valves, vented and the pilot lights turned off. The venting fuel could be used as a round out burn at the last moment if there is time.

If VHF radio is carried a May Day call should be made, time permitting, to alert emergency services.

Precautionary landing
This is a fully controlled landing made at the earliest convenient site following an incident. Normal landing procedures should be adopted. Even when an emergency situation has been dealt with and the aircraft is no longer in danger it is still advisable that a landing should be made at the earliest opportunity. Especially if the balloon is operating on only one instead of two fuel/burner systems.

Pilot Light Failure
If the pilot light fails on lift-off it is generally due to sudden windshear blowing it out. The gas is still flowing and re-ignition is simply a matter of

operating the burner ignition system or using an external source of spark or flame.

If the pilot light fails and attempts at re-ignition also fail, check that:–

a) the pilot light valve on the burner has not been turned off inadvertently
b) the quick release coupling on the vapour hose has not been released or unseated
c) the cylinder valve is fully opened

If these checks fail to reintroduce the flow of gas try fitting the vapour hose on another master cylinder, if one is carried.

Where there is a second fuel system with its own pilot light functioning use this but prepare to land at the earliest convenient opportunity.

If all else fails the main burner can be used without a pilot light for a short time. To do this, close the main valve on the cylinder to be used and fully open the burner valve to vent the line. The cylinder valve can then be opened just a fraction and the main burner lit with matches or sparker. Opening the valve will produce a normal main flame and leaving the valve open a fraction in between keeps it alight. Prolonged use in this fashion will lead to freezing around the valve so a landing must be carried out without delay.

There may be insufficient height to give enough time to try any remedies — in this case prepare immediately for an emergency landing.

Relighting the pilot light and the use of main burner without a pilot light are both exercises which can be practised on the ground until the student feels confident that they can be carried out efficiently in the air. Experienced pilots could also benefit from practice sessions from time to time.

Main burner failure
Nowadays most balloons have two independent fuel systems even if they do not have two burners, so if one system fails there is the second back-up to use while the failed system is investigated. Check that the main cylinder valve hasn't been closed accidentally and that the coupling has been fitted correctly. If there is still no flow of fuel change the hose to another cylinder if one is available. If no flow can be established at all continue on the alternative system and prepare to land as soon as possible.

If both systems or burners fail to operate, check all valves and couplings and switch hoses to other cylinders where possible. If a functioning burner system cannot be re-established prepare for an emergency landing. In this instance it may be possible to arrest a fast descent by the jettison of ballast (any loose equipment — gas cylinders etc.) providing this action will not endanger the lives of people on the ground.

Fire in the air
This is most likely to arise from a propane leak on or around the burner which is ignited when the burner is operated.

If this is the case the propane supply to the area of the fire must be shut down and the pilot light valve closed. Activate the fire extinguisher and aim it at the base of the flames. Once the fire is out, if the propane supply to the leaking area can be totally isolated the pilot light can be relit and a landing made at the earliest opportunity.

One of the commonest causes of a leak on a burner is at the stem of a rego valve due to a damaged o-ring. Other causes could be leaking joints which have not been resealed or tightened correctly after servicing, or dirt in the propane which prevents valves sealing or causes damage to sealing surfaces.

Another source of a fire on board is where a leak occurs at a cylinder connection. The cylinder valve needs to be closed immediately and in this situation a quick shut-down valve can have the advantage over a screw valve. It is still a wise precaution to close the pilot light valve to prevent re-ignition of the leak and the fire extinguisher should be used if the flames continue. If the hose can be reconnected to another cylinder, and no leaking occurs, the pilot light may be relit and a precautionary landing made, otherwise an emergency landing without the burner will be necessary.

In situations like these, where just a second or two can make all the difference between a small fire and an inferno, it is obviously an advantage for a pilot to wear a good pair of gloves and a fire resistant flying suit so that if necessary a hand can reach through flames to close down valves or taps. In some instances it will be possible to extinguish the fire entirely by smothering it by hand.

It also follows that the fire extinguisher must be instantly available for use and not in a position that requires any length of time to release it.

Some pilots also like to carry a fire blanket. This can be used to smother flames or as a shield for occupants while other actions are carried out.

If a fire cannot be dealt with in the air, an immediate landing and evacuation must be made.

Fire on the ground
If the fire arises from leaks in the fuel system, shout to get people to clear the area and turn off any open valves. Operate the fire extinguisher aiming at the base of the flames. Ask others to remove any other cylinders which may be outside the basket and to remove if possible any vehicles from the area. If the fire is not under control within thirty seconds everyone should totally evacuate the area and the emergency services be called in.

When inflating in dry conditions it is possible to ignite the grass in front of the burner and if the fan is running it can quickly spread. It is important therefore to remember to shut down the fan as well as the fuel lines in such a situation.

Bearing in mind that the basket will be on its side at a time like this and that the on-board extinguisher may not be so readily accessible, it is advisable to have another extinguisher available for use by the ground crew. Some balloonists have one mounted on the inflation fan or one that they carry in the retrieve vehicle which can be placed in a convenient place during inflation.

Contact with power lines
The general rule when overflying power lines is to have the envelope hot and climbing. However if contact with power lines appears unavoidable it

is advisable to make the contact as high up the envelope as possible. In this way the flying wires will not be caught up and the basket and the occupants will be closer to the ground. It is therefore more sensible in this case to rip out before the lines than to burn and make a futile attempt to clear them.

All fuel lines should be closed and vented if possible and the burner left untouched since contact with metal parts must be avoided. Passengers must be warned to hold on tightly and keep well down in the basket, while avoiding any contact with wires or metal. If the basket is suspended above the ground no-one should attempt to leave the basket, nor should anyone on the ground approach or attempt to free the balloon until the generating board is contacted and can confirm that all power is off.

A pilot should be aware that the basket or flying wires when in contact with power lines can be burnt through by the resultant arcing, which can tip the basket over and possibly eject the occupants.

Tree contact
Tree contact can be made when over-flying woods as a result of the pilot not being prepared for the 'cold sink' effect of the air mass over woods. If the balloon just settles into the tops of the trees then steady heat applied to the envelope should lift the balloon clear again. Care should be taken to ensure that the crown line, rip line and fuel hoses etc. do not entangle in the branches. If the balloon has any forward speed at this point, it should be remembered that the envelope may tip over as it tries to continue on its way making it difficult to direct heat into the mouth.

Although there is no scientific evidence to prove it, practice shows that a balloon will always be attracted to the single tree in a hedgerow or the tallest tree in a row! If there appears to be no chance of avoiding such a tree, then, as with power lines, contact is best made by the envelope with the basket being at the lowest point possible. Depending on the forward speed of the balloon and the type of tree, it may just be possible for the envelope to rotate around the tree until clear on the other side. Hold in all free lines and hoses to avoid them becoming caught around with branches. If the crown line, rip line or control line becomes caught it may be possible to release it by undoing the free end and letting it go. Providing there are no toggles or large carabiners on the ends which could wedge in branches the balloon could fly clear. Landing without access to the rip line could present another problem. (See Ripline/Parachute failure in this chapter.) Care should also be taken when operating the burner if there are branches close to which could catch alight.

If there is no chance of flying free, i.e. the envelope itself becomes impaled on branches, the pilot light should be turned off, the hoses vented and the situation assessed for evacuation of the basket and retrieval of the envelope from the tree. If the basket isn't too far from the ground it may be possible to use the handling line to climb down or the trees themselves, but it may be more sensible to wait until help is at hand on the ground to lend assistance. Where part of the balloon is firmly hooked on a branch or branches care should be taken when attempting to release it as branches which are suddenly freed can spring back up with quite a violent force.

Having got everyone safely on to terra firma the task of retrieving the envelope and basket must be tackled. Damage to the envelope often looks a lot worse than it actually is and more serious damage can be caused by trying to remove it without careful assessment of the situation. Obviously if any tree requires cutting down or branches removed the landowner must be consulted first.

Water contact

An uncomfortable rather than a major emergency. When flying over water a pilot can be caught out by the 'cold sink' effect found over large areas of water. It is also difficult to judge height over water and it is not uncommon for the basket to be inadvertently dunked in. A wicker basket does little to keep the water out and this can make leaving the water more difficult than imagined. To clear the surface the balloon needs to be able to lift not only its own weight but initially the weight of the water in the basket has to be overcome as well. Bearing in mind that a gallon of water weighs 10 lb it is easy to work out that a small heavily laden balloon may not be able to! If the balloon is able to clear the water the excess in the basket will quickly drain away and the flight can safely continue. If, however, the basket is not able to break free then where possible the envelope should be kept inflated to keep it out of the water whilst the basket is by some means navigated to the shore. Easier said than done, but not as difficult as trying to retrieve a water-laden envelope from the water as well.

Rip line/parachute failure

Failure of the rip line or failure of the parachute to function both give rise to the need to land without the ability to control descent by venting excess hot air. These types of malfunction are not very common and generally avoidable.

Rip line — Careful inspection of the rip line and its securing point and pulleys before inflation should reveal any areas likely to cause problems and remedial action taken. This together with careful inflation and pre take-off checks should ensure that the rip line will function correctly when needed.

However, a neglected line can fail in several ways. The securing loop sewn into the envelope could fail or the knotted end of the line become detached. In most cases this would not result in the entire line descending into the basket because there is generally a large bead or knots tied a few feet up from this end which will jam in the parachute pulley. The parachute would still function but the pull on the line required to operate it would be much greater. If any pulley becomes jammed the friction on the line as it is pulled through could generate sufficient heat to cause melting on the rope. This may not weaken it enough to break in the first instance but further neglect could result in the line failing when pulled. A common cause of a pulley jamming is loose threads left inside a balloon after repair work. These become tangled around the lines and transferred to the pulleys as they go through. The rip line can also be damaged by the burner on inflation weakening it sufficiently to break when tension is applied.

Parachute — Failure of the parachute to operate is usually related to some malfunction of the rip line — possibly only a small knot or tangle which jams the line in a pulley and which should be spotted before take-off. When this happens the take-off can be postponed until the envelope has been allowed to cool, pulled down by the crown line and the problem rectified.

If the situation is not discovered until the parachute is operated in flight, then a landing **without the use of the parachute** will be necessary. The envelope will have to cool naturally and sufficient time needs to be allowed for this to happen before the chosen landing site is reached. Once a descent is set up the rate can be controlled by the gentle application of small amounts of heat. The landing area will have to have sufficient space for the balloon to come to rest so the larger the better. If radio contact can be made with crew they could possibly be at an intended landing field and assist in slowing the basket down once on the ground.

A parachute which fails to close may not be spotted when inspected pre-take-off, though a clue to something amiss could be that the mouth of the envelope appears to be sucking in, indicating the possibility of air being lost through the top. The cause could be tangling or knotting of the spider or securing lines — a situation which may be resolved if the parachute is deployed and allowed to re-seat itself. Another cause could be shrunk or short securing lines which will prevent the parachute closing sufficiently to make a seal with the envelope. This could be due to getting the balloon wet — the effect of heat on damp lines can have the same shrinking effect as a tumbledryer does on some garments! With a leaking parachute the balloon will require far more heat to keep it airborne and a precautionary landing should be made at the earliest opportunity. If a balloon is not heavily laden yet seems to require excessive use of the burner to keep airborne it is wise to investigate the parachute seal.

Heatlink dropping
If the heatlink in the envelope reaches a set temperature it will part and the end with streamer attached will fall down into the basket. While not a state of emergency in itself it does indicate that there is more heat at that point in the envelope than is good for the fabric. If the burner is on at the time, and it is safe to do so it should be turned off to allow natural cooling to take place and the envelope should be examined on landing for signs of overheating of the fabric — discoloration or changes in texture, or indication on the temperature label that a high temperature has been experienced. Overheating can be caused by flying with too much weight in the basket or over-operation of the burner. Constant overheating will cause fabric to degrade more quickly and can shorten the life of an envelope quite considerably. A replacement heatlink should be fitted before the next flight.

Fabric damage
An envelope may be damaged before a flight either when last packed away, on laying out due to careless handling or sharp objects on the ground, or during the inflation itself. In these cases the damage is likely to be spotted during the pre take-off checks and can be rectified before flight. What can give cause for concern is when the envelope is damaged in flight. Following contact with trees or other objects the envelope should

always be examined for tears before deciding to continue the flight. Tears below the equator can generally be ignored unless they are very numerous or load tapes are also damaged. The area above the equator is one which does more 'work' and carries more stress than lower down. A tear here should only split as far as vertical or horizontal load tapes under normal flight stresses but heat will be constantly lost through such a hole and a precautionary landing will need to be made. More than one tear and the envelope will probably be unable to support its weight in the air. Small tears apparent before a flight but not treated in any way could well enlarge with worrying results once the envelope is under the stress of flight.

Propane leak
Indications of leaking fuel can be the smell of propane, hissing, or freezing around connectors/valves. If these signs can be spotted before fire is also involved an emergency situation can be averted. Thorough investigation should follow the discovery of any signs of leaking, followed by the isolation of the system at fault. If the fault is at a connector, removal and reconnection may be all that is necessary for a cure.

17

FUEL MANAGEMENT

Burner system

Although burners can differ in types and style — either as single or multiple units — generally they all operate on the same basic principles.

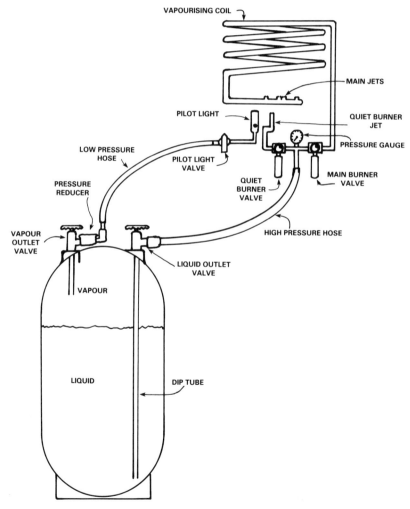

Fig. 17–1   A simple burner system

All burners carry a pilot light which burns throughout the flight to ignite the main flame. Most pilot lights operate on propane vapour and so require a separate hose to draw from the vapour outlet of a master fuel cylinder. There are some pilot lights which operate on liquid propane taken from the main burner feed and do not require a vapour supply.

Main burner
The main burner needs a much larger volume of vapour to burn than could be drawn from a cylinder without giving rise to problems of freezing and pressure. It therefore draws from the liquid take-off valve on a cylinder. This connection has a long dip-tube reaching almost to the base of the cylinder and will draw liquid until the level in the tank drops below the tube level. When the burner valve is opened liquid propane passes through the burner coil to the main jets, where the pilot light provides ignition. The heat from the flame vaporises the propane in the coil which in turn provides the large quantity of vapour needed to produce the typical efficient 'blue' roaring flame. The greater the pressure of the liquid propane passing into the coils the greater the flame and therefore the heat output.

Quiet burner
Most burner assemblies these days are fitted with some type of quiet burner to be used when overflying livestock or other areas sensitive to noise. This is generally a single large jet which burns straight liquid propane and is a much quieter yellow flame.

Fig. 17–2   Insulated tank cover

Cylinders

It is important when inflating that the cylinders to be used are in the correct orientation to feed appropriate hoses, i.e. liquid to a liquid feed hose and vapour to a vapour one. However once a cylinder is lying horizontally the liquid dip tube could be in the vapour space and the vapour take-off could be below the liquid level. Unfortunately there is no consistent cylinder valve configuration to make this task easy. Usually there are labels on the cylinders to indicate which way they should lie on their sides to provide liquid or vapour. Only two cylinders at most need to be orientated for inflation since only one liquid and one vapour feed should be activated at this time.

All cylinders must be firmly secured in the basket, even if a cylinder is only to be used for inflation and left behind at take-off. Most baskets have provision for each cylinder to be retained by two straps. A cylinder will be more secure if the top strap is fastened above the shoulder of the tank.

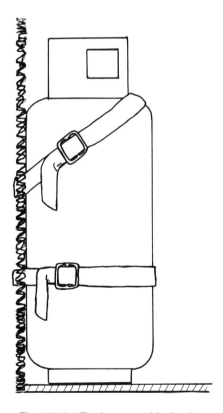

Fig. 17–3   Tank secured in basket

Burner pressure will depend on the pressure of the propane in the cylinders. In cold weather this pressure will be considerably reduced resulting in a much smaller, less powerful flame. There are ways in which

pressure can be increased in a cylinder to overcome this. Some balloonists get round the problem by introducing nitrogen, under pressure, into
the the vapour space. Obviously, this can only be done to cylinders which
do not have a vapour take-off if they are needed to run a pilot light.
Alternatively the cylinders can be heated to increase their pressure. Hot
water poured over an uncovered tank can be very effective especially if the
cylinder is then fitted with a well insulated cover. It is possible to use
special electrical jackets which work on an electric blanket principle but
there is some doubt as to the wisdom of mixing propane and electricity
from a safety point of view. There have been rumours of pilots taking
cylinders to bed with them to get their temperatures up — or at least
taking them indoors on cold winter nights, neither method to be recommended in the interests of safety!

Fuel management
During flight it is important to be aware of the fuel levels at all times.
The fuel gauge on a cylinder starts to read as the contents fall below
35%–30%. It is usually good practice to burn off the master cylinder first
since a pilot light drawing vapour continuously will cause the temperature

Fig. 17–4   Flight cylinder showing fuel gauge

to drop in this tank. Some fuel must be left to provide vapour for the pilot
light — usually about 10%. It should be noted that some burner configur-
ations may require the quiet burner also to operate from the master
cylinder and sufficient fuel will need to be left in the cylinder to allow the
use of this burner. An important factor if only two cylinders are carried.

Where more than two cylinders are carried, a pilot must also be prepared to change over from empty to full cylinders. One system must be operational at all times so there should never be more than one hose uncoupled. The balloon should be hot and climbing when preparing to relocate a main hose, to allow time for the change-over. The cylinder valve must be closed, and the line vented by burning. The hose can then be removed and coupled to a full cylinder. When the cylinder's main valve is opened, a routine check for leaks should be carried out before the system is function tested by a single burn.

If a note is made of the duration of the first cylinder, a rough calculation can be made to indicate how long the remaining fuel on board will last. It is good practice to look for a landing site with approximately thirty minutes fuel in hand (or 20% of original quantity).

18

APPROACH & OVERSHOOT/LANDING

Every flight has to come to an end whatever the duration or course taken which ideally means choosing a convenient landing field somewhere ahead, making an approach into this field, and rounding out of the descent in time for the balloon to come gently to a halt at ground level! However there will be the occasion when the approach has to be aborted and an 'overshoot' carried out.

Included in the flight exercises for a student pilot are 'approach and overshoot from high level' and 'approach and overshoot from low level'.

For any approach an important aspect is the **choice of field**. This field must be large enough for the balloon to come safely to rest. Obviously, the greater the balloon's forward speed the more length it will need to come to a halt. Ideally the field must be clear of obstacles on the approach and should not contain livestock or crop which could be damaged on landing. The area should also be clear of telephone or power lines. Check too for features of the landscape such as a sharp decline which could overturn the basket. It is always helpful if the chosen field is close to a road or good track.

Pre-landing checks
Having selected a landing field a pilot must then run through the pre-landing checks.

Using the mnemonic **B.E.F.O.R.E.** as an aid to memory:—

Brief passengers.
The briefing given to passengers on take-off concerning landing should be repeated, especially for the benefit of new, first time flyers who will probably have forgotten every word you said before take-off.

Instruct passengers to have knees slightly bent on landing to help absorb the impact and avoid the chance of spinal or other injuries. It is better not to face forward but rather to be backwards or sideways on to the direction of landing. Holding on in two separate places is steadier than having both hands on the same hand-hold. It must be stressed that arms and hands must be kept within the basket when landing. Anything outside at this time stands a chance of being caught under the basket rim with the likelihood once more of serious injuries. It must be stressed that no-one may leave the basket without the pilot's permission — at any time.

Equipment stowed and secure.
All items need to be safely stowed prior to landing to prevent them

causing injury to people on board in the event of a heavy touch-down and also to prevent objects being lost overboard on landing.

Fuel sufficient for landing and overshoot.
Never attempt an approach on a near empty tank, when loss of pressure could give a greatly reduced flame, and which probably would not give enough lift at the right time if an overshoot is necessary.

Obstacles — approach and overshoot clear.

Rip line to hand.
Because it is easy to become disorientated with rotation of the balloon in flight the rip line may not be in the position you think, so frequently check its location during flight so that you can put your hand on it instantly at this point.

Establish descent.

Descent
Having selected a landing field a rate of descent must be set up which will bring the balloon to the ground at the chosen point. Parallax can be a very useful way of achieving this. It may be necessary to use the rip line to

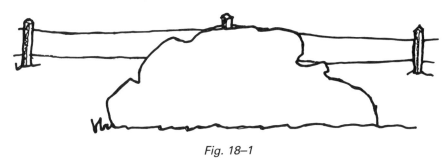

Fig. 18–1

initiate the descent. Only hold the parachute vent open for a few seconds and wait for the delayed reaction.
    A point is selected for touch down and its relation to another object

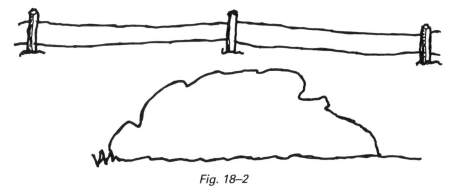

Fig. 18–2

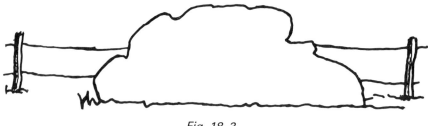

Fig. 18–3

between the balloon and this point is noted. As long as this relationship is maintained the balloon is at the correct angle of descent.

If the relative distance between the two points increases the rate of descent needs to be increased.

If the distance decreases an undershoot is likely and the descent needs to be slightly arrested.

This method of descending to a chosen point works for both high and low level approaches. However, because the rate of descent is greater in a high level approach it is not as easy to control as an approach from low level. Any subsequent overshoot will also require more heat to arrest a fast descent from high level.

Approach from low level

A low level approach should be chosen where possible. It is more controlled because of the gentle rate of descent. This is done with a warm envelope, kept under control by frequent short bursts of heat. Because the envelope is kept warm it is easy to arrest the descent and make a climb out should the landing need to be aborted. A gentle touch down is also easier to execute if the vertical speed of the balloon is very low.

Approach from high level

There may be times when a low approach is not possible, and a much steeper angle of descent will be needed for the approach. The landing field may have obstructions on the upwind boundary or there may be livestock to be overflown before the landing field is reached. Speed may be such that height is needed to see far enough ahead to select a suitable landing field. It could be that landing is a last minute decision taken at height with a fast descent necessary to achieve it.

Overshoot

As soon as it is apparent that the landing site is not suitable the descent must be arrested and a climb out initiated. The reasons for an overshoot are various — sudden changes of direction as low level is reached resulting in missing the chosen landing spot altogether or being right in line for the huge oak tree on the field boundary — the appearance of livestock into the field — the realisation that what looked like rough pasture from a few hundred feet is in fact standing crop.

The rate of climb out again will be determined by conditions and the downwind obstacles. If there is the likelihood of landing almost immediately it may be possible to maintain the flight at low level in readiness for this. On the other hand there may be the need for a steep climb out, especially if there are high downwind obstacles, i.e power lines, to be cleared.

Landing

If everything is going according to plan on the approach for a landing, with no need for an overshoot, all the pilot needs to do is **round out** of the descent so that the balloon has no vertical speed as it touches the ground.

Judging just when to round out is no easy operation and depends on many different factors. No two balloons will respond the same when trying to halt a descent. The size of the balloon, burner output, weight carried, fuel pressure can all have an influence on the rate at which a descent can be arrested and so it is a simple case of trial and error to get things right. Basically what needs to be done is that the descent needs to be stopped by a roundout burn which ends at such a height that all that is then needed is for the rip to be held open as the balloon touches the ground.

Ideally on the roundout burn the pilot light should be closed down at the burner valve, or 'popped' at the cylinder connection and the fuel lines also closed down at the cylinder thereby venting the lines with this last burn.

It is good safe practice to ensure that the pilot light is always out before the balloon has ground contact. With lots of things happening at this point it is necessary to eliminate the chance of causing ignition either to the field or the balloon. It is a very quick matter to relight the pilot light should there be a need for further burner use once the balloon is on the ground.

19

AFTER FLIGHT

Arriving gently back on the ground after a pleasant flight (or as sometimes happens, in a tangle of arms and legs, rattling across a field in a basket on its side hoping it will very soon come to a standstill) may mark the end of the flying, but there are still tasks to be done and procedures to follow before the customary retirement to the nearest bar or breakfast place.

In whatever situation you find yourself, no-one must leave the basket until the pilot is satisfied that loss of weight from the basket will not cause further movement of the balloon.

In the case of a stand-up landing; when the pilot is certain there is no buoyancy left he may instruct a passenger to step out and take the crown line in readiness for pulling the envelope down for deflation. If it will assist the retrieve crew to locate the landing site, a pilot may decide to keep the envelope inflated. In this case the pilot light will have to be relit and the envelope kept warm with short bursts of heat. This can only be done if there is little or no wind to move the envelope around and when the landing field is free of obstacles which could hazard the envelope if there was any unexpected movement.

It may sometimes be possible for the still inflated balloon to be 'walked' to the field gateway or edge near a road to make packing up and loading the retrieve vehicle or trailer an easier task. With only the pilot on board keeping the envelope on the point of buoyancy passengers can guide the balloon to the desired position for deflation.

Fig. 19–1   Walk out

The pilot should not vacate the basket until the burner/fuel system is safely shut down and all lines vented. If the pilot light has been relit it should be turned off and all lines should be closed at the cylinder. The lines can then be cleared or vented by opening the burner valves. Do ensure that no-one is smoking before doing this and that the burner is pointing away from people and envelope. It can save on replacement batteries if the instrument pack is switched off before leaving the basket too.

To deflate the envelope the rip line is operated while the crown line is pulled out in a downwind direction. (Trying to deflate across the wind usually causes the envelope to form a huge sail and a great deal more effort is needed to pull it down.) As the envelope comes to rest it may be necessary to lay the basket over on its side to take strain off the burner frame and upright poles. Once the basket is on its side, the deflation may be speeded up by having the mouth of the envelope held closed and someone working along from the mouth, funnelling the envelope and driving out the trapped air in the process.

If the basket tips over on landing the rip should be held open to enable the air to leave the envelope as quickly as possible. When safe to do so someone should be instructed by the pilot to close the mouth of the balloon to prevent more air being taken in and prolonging deflation. As before, the fuel system should be made safe before the basket is left unattended and the instrument pack switched off.

When the air is out of the envelope the flying wires can be disconnected from the burner frame, hoses uncoupled from cylinders and the basket rigging dismantled. Before hoses are uncoupled, check again that the

Fig. 19–2   Burner with hoses secured for transit

burner system has been vented and the hoses cleared. The envelope wires may be loosely coiled to prevent tangling. Tight coils can put strain on wires that have been overheated giving them permanent 'kinks'.

Burner hoses should not be allowed to drag when the burner is carried to the retrieve vehicle. Some form of tie is a good idea to fasten them to the burner frame where they are not in danger of being trapped or damaged in other ways. Covers or caps to keep dust and dirt out of the hose connectors are a sensible idea. (The same applies to cylinder valve connections.)

If the envelope bag is carried the envelope can now be packed away. Starting at the crown, some people prefer to partially roll their envelope before packing the rest on top while others opt to feed the whole lot in the bag without rolling up the first few feet. Whatever method is adopted the crown line should be coiled and carefully laid on the envelope a short distance from the top to avoid the chance of it becoming tangled in the free load tapes and crownring. The flying wires should be the last things into the bag, carefully wrapped in the Nomex skirt or scoop to prevent damage to the nylon.

If the retrieve crew has found the balloon it is often a good idea to let them continue packing away while the pilot endeavours to find the land-owner. Do not drive vehicles onto private land without permission. Pack up the equipment and carry it all out to the roadside if the landowner cannot be found or permission is not given.

Spectators can often get carried away in their excitement at seeing a balloon land and it is often advisable to post someone to discourage them from entering the landing field if it is private property. Well-meaning helpers can often inflict more damage than a balloon to crops or property, but the balloonists are still to blame in the eyes of the farmer.

If the retrieve crew appears to be lost and there is no radio contact then a telephone should be found once all the packing up is complete and instructions left for them to locate the landing field. A map reference is usually left to simplify matters. Of course this remedy can only be carried out if a common retrieve telephone number has previously been agreed between the air and ground crews!

When everything is packed away it is wise to cast an eye around to check that nothing has been left behind. Small objects can often be shot out of the basket on landing, igniters, pens etc. Before leaving do make sure that all gates, and anything else which has been moved or removed are left as found.

Other after flight actions must include preparing the balloon for the next flight — i.e. refuelling and rectifying any defects, and also completing entries in the relevant logbooks.

20

TETHERING

There are several methods of tethering, but whether the wind is one knot or fifteen knots the same principles should apply. Remember, if the balloon is certified for tethering in surface winds up to fifteen knots then tethering in faster conditions will invalidate your CofA and probably your insurance cover. Assuming that conditions are satisfactory, the main requirement is to limit the amount of travel that the balloon may make.

Connections to the balloon are invariably made to the load frame/flying wire/basket wire junctions. The methods are down to the individual manufacturers and each suggests their preferred connection points and method in their balloon manuals. Suffice to say that usually a form of 'V' bridle, generally made of substantial stainless steel wire rope, is connected by carabiners to these points. A single carabiner at the base of the 'V' is the point at which tether ropes may be connected. (Note that a quick release attachment and tether 'V' bridle are not the same thing.) 5000 kg carabiners should be used for the bridle and tether connections (standard flying carabiners are usually 2500 kg). Tether ropes ought to have a breaking strength of at least four tonnes. Handling lines are not usually strong enough for tether use.

Good solid fixed tether points in the form of mature trees are not always convenient but if they are, use them in preference to vehicles. However, vehicles (the heavier the better) make a reasonable substitute and have the distinct advantage of being moveable to the ideal positions dictated by the wind direction at the tether site. Fixture points on the vehicle must be suitable for the task — i.e. towing eyes or better still, properly mounted winches, etc. It is poor practice to attach tethers to the rear of trailers. These can move independently of the towing vehicle and may possibly become disconnected from same if shifted violently.

It makes sense for vehicles used to be parked in gear with the brakes applied. Bear in mind that even a relatively heavy vehicle can slide across wet grass quite easily, especially if it is a sloping site!

The aim of the tether lines is to restrain the balloon's horizontal and vertical movement. Horizontal movement can be controlled by having a three-point tether arrangement — i.e lines going out at approximately 120° to each other. Vertical movement can be controlled by the length of the tether lines, and the amount of slack in the downwind line in particular. The two upwind lines are fixed, with the third, being more of a controlling line than a tether, usually attached to the front of the load frame assembly. Although left slack for control it is a sensible safety precaution to have the end of this line also fixed to a vehicle or fixture. Some pilots may use an additional downwind control line for extra stability.

The prime consideration in all tethering operations is safety. Crew must

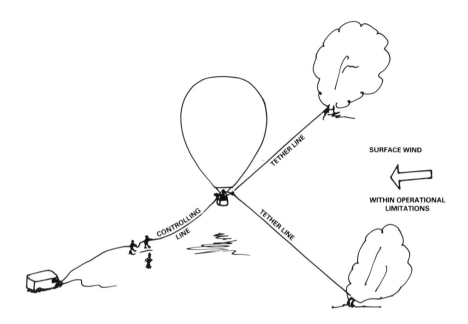

Fig. 20–1   Tether line arrangement

be well briefed and there must be a safe clearance between spectators and the balloon (including its tether lines). The safest place for spectators is upwind of the balloon.

Ground crew should be made well aware of the dangers involved when tethering — especially when working around ropes which are under tension.

To be in command of the situation, crew need to keep excess slack out of the control line(s) so that when the situation arises where their weight is required on the line it can be immediately applied. If there is excessive slack the momentum gained as the balloon takes it up can produce a snatching action on the line and crew can lose control. Any crew handling lines must wear suitable gloves to avoid the danger of rope burns to the hands.

Remember the golden rules for crews:
- — **nobody at any time should allow themselves to be lifted off their feet.**
- — **no rope or control line etc. attached to the balloon should be twisted around hands or other parts of the body.**

Additional safety measures when tethering are:
- — **keep a watchful eye on the balloon's movement at all times.**
- — **never stand directly beneath the basket.**
- — **do not stand on or step over the tether lines.**

Tethered flying

The balloon should be laid out for inflation as usual, and the tether lines attached before any air is admitted to the envelope. The quick release restraint may be used, especially if the balloon is not laid out at the extent of the upwind tether lines.

As for any inflation, although free flight is not the intention in this case, the balloon should be equipped and ready for such a contingency.

Once the balloon is upright and the pre take-off checks made the quick release can be freed and the balloon walked downwind to the extent of the upwind tether lines.

The pilot needs to lift the balloon off the ground very gently to avoid

(Thunder & Colt)

Fig. 20–2   Tethering

snatching on the tether lines as limits are reached. In this manner the balloon can be allowed to round out and then kept buoyant by 'little and often' use of the burner. Similarly the balloon should be allowed to to come down at a very slow rate of descent.

As well as flying the balloon, a pilot also has to be aware of external factors when tethering. A constant watch must be kept on the tethers and the flight curtailed if the vehicles are seen to be moved or lifted; or if the crew are unable to handle their control line(s). Give warning to crew or other people who appear to be under the basket or too close to the lines or tethers.

It is helpful if there is sufficient crew available to have one or two standing by ready to step forward to hold the basket down when it touches the ground at the end of the flight or to exchange passengers. The pilot should remind passengers to have their knees slightly bent when about to touch down, and that no-one must leave the basket until asked to do so. If exchanging passengers it must be done in the order of 'one in' before 'one out'.

Tethered flying is an excellent way for a student to learn fine burner control. It can also be an opportunity to practice emergency procedures such as pilot light failure; relighting the pilot light and also using the main burner without the use of a pilot flame. (See Chapter 16: Emergency Procedures.)

When the balloon is at the top of its tether, further use of the burner can raise the envelope temperature above normal operating limits. It is, therefore, very easy to overheat an envelope whilst tethering and so accelerate degradation of the fabric. There is also an increased risk of burn damage to the mouth of the envelope because airflow across the burner is continually trying to push the flame downwind.

A scoop can be very useful when tethering. Not only does it assist by making inflation easier but once the balloon is airborne it continues to direct air into the envelope keeping it pressurised and more stable.

Tethering, with regard to its limitations, and the carriage of passengers is a subject currently under review by the CAA and BBAC Flying Committee. For up-to-date information a pilot should consult the relative article of the Air Navigation Order (ANO).

BBAC Pilots Circular also carries reports from the Flying Committee on their dealings with the CAA.

SECTION 3

GROUND STUDIES

21

LANDOWNER RELATIONS

The inevitable conclusion of any balloon flight is a landing that will have to be made, usually without permission, on someone else's property. It is therefore in the interests of every balloonist to make these unannounced visits as amicable as possible. Understandably, some farmers/landowners do not take very kindly to balloons dropping in on their private property with the attendant possibilities of crop, livestock, power supply or boundary damage. For this reason the British Balloon and Airship Club, liaising with the National Farmers' Union (NFU), created a code of conduct for balloon pilots to follow. The **BBAC: Pilot code of conduct** was drawn up in 1979 and updated March 1990.

The importance of this is emphasised by the fact that it is now a requirement for all student pilots to attend a 'Landowners Relations Course' before they can complete their training. These are arranged by the BBAC in the various regions.

The BBAC also introduced a listing of **sensitive areas** or prohibited zones (PZ's) with frequent updates to inform pilots of areas to avoid when landing (usually because of valuable livestock, unfriendly farmers, or those who demand landing fees) or areas to fly over at specific heights to avoid upsetting livestock. These areas need to be marked up on the Ordnance Survey 1:50,000 map for the region being flown. Other areas are sometimes included in competition ballooning and these together with the sensitive areas on the competition maps go under the title of Prohibited Competition Zones (PCZ's).

The updated lists of sensitive areas are published regularly in *Pilots' Circular*.

While it is in the interests of ballooning and airmanship for every pilot to follow this code of conduct, it is also in our interests for crews to be aware of the code. Often the retrieve crew from their position on the ground are the first point of contact with the farmer or landowner, so they too have an important part to play in the fostering of good relations with the farming community. It must be the pilot's responsibility to ensure that his crew are familiar with the code.

BBAC: PILOT CODE OF CONDUCT

Introduction
If we are to continue to enjoy our sport, it is vital that we retain the goodwill of farmers and landowners. Balloonists are reminded that the countryside is the farmers' livelihood. Grass is a crop, animals are easily frightened and farmers depend on electricity supplies for many purposes

We all recognise that if we land unasked on somebody's field the farmer is, albeit sometimes unwillingly, our host. Certain responsibilities follow from this, the most important of which are listed here.

This code is intended to be a reminder of the conduct that the BBAC and NFU expects from all pilots and must be followed at all times.

All balloonists should have insurance cover of a minimum of £250,000 for damage sustained by farmers and other third parties. In some cases, even this figure may be inadequate.

No-one should participate in organised events without evidence of adequate insurance, and it is the organisers' responsibility to check that all foreign balloonists have insurance cover which is effective in Great Britain.

1 FLIGHT PLANNING
1.1 Do not fly unless you are reasonably certain that your flight path will be over country which is suitable for landing. For example, in July/ August you should avoid flying over large areas of standing corn in light wind conditions.
1.2 Pilots flying outside their usual area should contact the relevant landowner liaison officer before flying and after the flight give him any information which may be useful to other pilots. In the case of balloon meets, the organisers should do this on behalf of pilots.
1.3 Organisers of balloon meets should include a reference to the code of conduct in their literature and should mention the code at briefings.

2 TAKE OFF
2.1 Always obtain permission from the landowner before driving on to the field.
2.2 Check that during the climb-out immediately downwind of the take-off site the balloon will not have to fly low over livestock. Remember animals in adjacent fields can be easily frightened.
2.3 Brief your crew and other helpers regarding closing of field gates.
2.4 Climb to above 500 ft as soon as possible to avoid unseen animals downwind.

3 IN THE AIR
3.1 Flying below 500 ft should be indulged in only when it is reasonably certain that there is no livestock concealed in the possible flight path. Use of the liquid fire burner is recommended below 500 ft. Many farm buildings contain livestock that may be disturbed by a low flying balloon. This is true all the year round, but particularly so during the winter months.
3.2 If it appears that livestock have been disturbed for any reason, note the location of the incident and check the cause with the farmer after landing. If you cannot locate the farm, inform the local Police station or telephone the local NFU Secretary. (See local telephone directory.)

4 THE LANDING AND RETRIEVE
4.1 Select a landing field that should cause the least possible inconvenience to the landowner. Particular care should be taken during the summer months when growing or standing crops, including hay,

cover large areas of the countryside and remember the grave risk of fire.

4.2 Ensure that the ground below and ahead is clear of livestock, overhead power lines, buildings or other property that could be damaged.

4.3 If an emergency dictates a choice between landings in crop or disturbing animals, opt if possible for the former. The damage to crop is likely to be minimal, and easily assessed. This is not so for livestock.

4.4 Immediately after landing, take all responsible steps to discourage onlookers from coming into the field and trespassing on the farmer's property. Avoid landing close to housing estates. The damage caused by third parties may be considerable.

4.5 Never make tethered flights or re-inflate the balloon in your landing field or carry out an intermediate landing unless you have obtained permission from the farmer.

4.6 Ensure that all farm gates are left as you found them.

4.7 Contact the landowner or farmer as soon as possible after landing. Obtain permission before allowing any vehicles to drive on to the field. Always leave a card recording your name, address, balloon registration and retrieve vehicle number.

4.8 If the landowner or farmer cannot be contacted after landing, you must leave your card with his agent or at his farm, obtain his name, address and telephone number and contact him as soon as possible afterwards.

4.9 If damage is caused or the farmer wishes to take further action ensure you record his name, address and telephone number and ask the farmer to write to you at the address on your card. Remember that you should be insured.

Landowner Relations Officers

The BBAC Regions each appoint a Landowner Relations Officer (LRO) to co-ordinate the publishing of the sensitive areas as they arise. Formerly known as NFU Liaison Officers, the BBAC magazine **AEROSTAT** lists each region's officer and telephone number in every issue. These officers liaise with the local NFU secretaries and their help or advice can be sought if a pilot has a farmer problem he is unable to resolve.

It is advisable to inform the LRO of any problem in his/her region even if it can be resolved without his help. It may be desirable to designate the location as a sensitive area for the benefit of other pilots.

When planning to fly in an unknown area, a pilot should contact the local LRO to check on the current sensitive area locations. The LRO is then also aware of another balloon in the region should there be any queries later.

Balloon Meet organisers should also liaise with LRO's before planning meets to ensure the information they may send to visiting pilots is up to date regarding sensitive area information.

No-one wishes to impose unnecessary restrictions in their local flying area but sometimes the designation of a location as a sensitive area before any trouble arises can be beneficial to both landowner and pilots. This especially applies to areas where livestock damage could be very costly, such as stud farms, chicken or turkey rearing sheds, or intensive pig units. (Often places which are not obvious from the air.)

The pilot code, paragraph 3.2, asks pilots to return to check with farmers when animals appear to have been upset. Another occasion where it may be a good idea to return to the farmer is when an obviously dead animal has been seen from the air. The farmer may not be aware of its demise and inspecting a cold stiff animal with the pilot only a short time after his flight could definitely rule out the balloon as the cause of death. Left until later there may be no way of telling what caused it and if the balloon had been noted it could be considered an obvious culprit.

Some pilots carry a camera in the basket all the time and are therefore able to take photographs of damage caused by or which could be attributed to his/her balloon, for their insurers. 'Disposable' cameras, which are bought complete with film for only a little more than the cost of a film, can be a useful item to keep in the basket for this purpose.

A pilot questioned by CAA officials or local police on landing, or at some later time after the flight, is strongly recommended to seek advice from the BBAC before answering any questions or making any statement.

To put things into perspective it must be said that, on the whole, the members of the farming community balloonists most frequently come into contact with are extremely friendly and helpful. Some will turn up in tractors to save carry-outs when the landing place is too muddy for retrieve vehicles, and others will offer hospitality while waiting for retrieve to turn up. Farmers who live in very isolated areas are often delighted to have new faces to talk to and packing up can turn into quite a lengthy social occasion. Crews can return home laden with fresh produce and invitations to 'land here whenever you like'. All these things add to the pleasure of a good flight.

It is a good idea to carry either in the vehicle or basket a small gift for a helpful farmer. Very few will object to a bottle of wine or spirits and on some occasions even a farmer who does not seem very happy about a balloon landing in his field can change his opinion of balloonists on receipt of one of these. Some sponsored balloons have sponsors samples to give away and other popular handouts, especially for the excited children who appear from nowhere, are photographs, badges or stickers.

Some BBAC regions, balloon meets, or competition events organise farmers' draws. The landing card with pilot's details is part of a draw ticket and having given the farmer his portion, the counterfoil with the farmer's name and address is entered into a draw which takes place at regular intervals in the region, or at the end of the balloon meet or competition.

Finally, an important point to bear in mind. The first impression a farmer gets of you can set the tone of the whole encounter. Leaning casually on the basket, hands in pockets, watching the farmer come towards you is not a good approach — go to him, handshake ready, introduce yourself, and apologise for the intrusion.

22

THE RETRIEVE

Having launched the balloon, what next? The ground crew stand in a small group looking upwards as P1 and his passengers wave and shout a belated thanks to everyone. Assuming that one of the pilot's pre-flight checks was to ensure that the retrieve driver had charge of the vehicle keys (it is surprising just how many times P1 takes to the air with them safely in his pocket) then the ground crew now have to organise themselves to carry out the task of following the balloon to its landing place where they can help to pack the whole outfit away. This is not such an easy task as it sounds!

Before any remaining equipment is packed away and secured in the vehicle or trailer it is advisable to take a bearing of the balloon as it flies away. Knowing the direction of flight will help in the initial choice of route for the retrieve crew to follow. Without the balloon in the vehicle or trailer care must be taken to secure loose items to avoid damage. Spare cylinders should travel upright to avoid damage to dip-tubes, securely tied or strapped in position. The fan must also be secured and checked to ensure that its petrol supply has been turned off.

When leaving the launch site remember to leave gates as found.

Hopefully, the retrieve vehicle will be equipped with a complete set of Ordnance Survey maps for the area being flown. Following a balloon using just a road atlas or no maps at all can be difficult, if not impossible. It can be extremely useful if the retrieve maps, like the flying maps, are also marked up with the BBAC sensitive areas and air information. It can be helpful to know when the balloon is crossing sensitive areas or perhaps an air traffic zone, when it would be unlikely to land. If the balloon lands near to a sensitive area the crew can avoid the area too and prevent further upset with a landowner.

To some extent, windspeed governs the type of route the retrieve will need to follow, although the basic idea is the same on any retrieve — to follow as close to the balloon as possible and to be nearby when it lands.

A slow retrieve

In calm conditions there should be sufficient time to plot the approximate flight direction on the map and to pinpoint the track more exactly, by arranging to be close when the balloon crosses points on the road for example. There may be time at road junctions and crossroads to study the map and decide on the best routes, and if you have taken a wrong turning or the balloon has changed direction there will probably be time to back-track and try another route. It is not a good plan to get too far ahead of the balloon as it can change direction or even land without warning and valuable time can be lost backtracking and trying to find it again.

Radio communication between balloon and retrieve can save a lot of wasted time, but over use of it can make a retrieve crew lazy. If R/T is used as a means of directing the retrieve crew's every move the skill is taken out of the exercise, together with some of the fun and enjoyment. (It is also not the intended use for which a radio operators licence is granted.) A good pilot will therefore only use radio to contact his retrieve to let them know if he is about to do anything which could affect their choice of route, i.e. if he is going to overfly a large built-up area, cross a river with few road bridges, attempt a final approach or if he has landed.

On a retrieve when there is time to pause and take stock, do not stop without ensuring that other road users will not be inconvenienced. Watch out for other drivers too who, on seeing a balloon at close quarters are prone to making sudden stops, often in the middle of narrow country lanes. Quite often they will then leave the vehicle to take photographs or videos oblivious to any other traffic on the road.

During a slow retrieve the crew will often be stopped by other followers and asked a wide variety of questions. These often illustrate just how little the public understand about hot air ballooning, for example . . .

'Where will the balloon land?'
'What time will it be coming back?'
'He's coming down, has he run out of lift?'
'Why doesn't he land in that nice field over on his left/right?'
'Hope he hasn't run out of sand bags.'
'What will happen if it gets a puncture?'

It can save time to have a few answers already worked out!

Often the answers crews themselves get to their questions are not as helpful as they could be.

'Have you seen a balloon land in this area?' has prompted the reply, 'Yes, about three weeks ago last Sunday.'

When asked about a balloon of a specific colour it is surprising how many folk cannot remember the colour, or they mention some colour which only appears on the balloon in a very small quantity and doesn't sound at all like the envelope you are supposed to be retrieving.

A fast retrieve

In faster windspeeds the crew really has to be on their toes. A bearing needs to be taken on the balloon as soon as it is airborne, before it disappears out of sight — and the crew has to pack the gear away and get on the road as quickly as possible.

In these conditions it is recommended that one person is nominated the navigator. This person should have a good knowledge of O.S maps and map-reading so that the driver can be given clear directions as each junction is reached. It must be appreciated that long straight roads rarely lie directly beneath the balloon's track and that consequently the retrieve vehicle will have to travel somewhere in the region of six times the distance covered by the balloon.

It therefore follows that retrieve will have to travel at a faster speed than the balloon in order to keep up with it, so it is sensible in fast conditions to avoid small country lanes and to travel on main roads as close as possible to the balloon's track in order to be anywhere near at the time of landing.

In really fast conditions, or if windspeed increases, chances are the balloon will become a mere speck on the horizon, which, just as the crew think they are drawing closer, suddenly disappears from sight, never to be seen again!

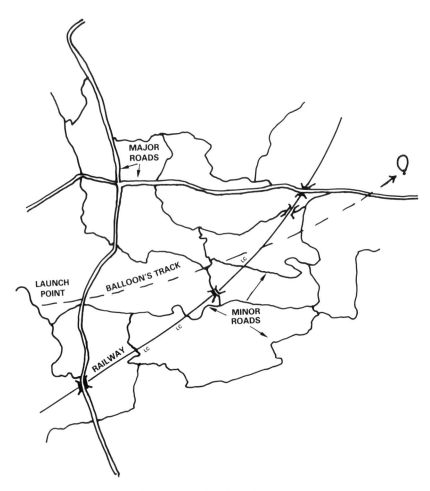

Fig. 22–1 Choice of route

As the above map demonstrates, when the balloon is travelling at speed, the main roads are the better choice for retrieve. In slow conditions there would be the option of taking the minor roads and getting under the balloon's track on several occasions. Hold-ups at level crossings would not be too important in slow conditions either as there would be time to catch up with the balloon.

Retrieve in general

Without radio contact how can a retrieve crew know what the pilot is planning to do? Often P1 will give the crew some idea of the length of flight he intends to make, so if he appears to be making an approach after this time chances are that he is landing. However it has to be realised that nothing is as unpredictable as a balloon flight and plans can change even at the very last moment. An approach for a landing may have to be aborted if animals are suddenly spotted in the chosen field, or if a previously hidden power line comes into view.

If the pilot is hoping to do an intermediate landing to exchange passengers, he may arrange simple signals to let the ground crew know his wishes — i.e. waving both arms could mean 'come to me'; both hands on head could mean 'bring me a full fuel cylinder'. In such cases the pilot will hopefully have made his intermediate landing in a place where the crew are able to get to him easily. As when the balloon makes a final landing, retrieve vehicles should not be driven on to private property without permission.

A balloon maintaining a reasonable height and with regular use of the cow-burner — the clearly visible, yellow flame which is much quieter than the main burner — probably means that the pilot is over livestock of some kind and is doing his best not to disturb them. It is unlikely therefore that a landing will be anticipated until the balloon has cleared the area.

Sometimes on a flight the balloon can take on a very distorted shape which looks rather disturbing from the ground. It may also appear to be rotating. These can be indications that the pilot is carrying out a 'cold descent'. The balloon has been allowed to cool down and is descending so rapidly that distortion is inevitable. It should be pointed out that this manoeuvre looks far worse from the ground than it does from the basket and is the recognised way to descend quickly from height. Similar effects can be observed if the balloon is making a rapid ascent.

The transition from a slow windstream level to a faster one or vice versa can also give rise to envelope distortion as can vigorous thermal activity.

It is helpful if the retrieve crew actually see the balloon touch down. A bearing can be taken on its position, even if it is some distance away, which can help in its subsequent location. When the crew are watching an approach at close quarters one way of deciding whether this is the landing or not is to watch the envelope for signs that the pilot is operating the rip line. When the rip line is pulled in, one of the first things to happen is that the attachment points for both the rope and the rip pulley location dimple in the sides of the balloon. Often the pilot can be seen to be pulling the line in, and if the balloon is viewed from higher ground the actual parachute can be seen to be pulled in to the envelope.

Sometimes it will be possible for the pilot to keep the balloon inflated once it has landed to enable the crew to locate it more easily. However, if there is too much forward speed to kill, the envelope is often dragged along by the wind, ahead of the basket, while the occupants cling on for dear life and wait for everything to come to a halt. This again is something which looks far worse to a spectator on the ground than to those taking part! Passers-by can think that things have gone terribly wrong, so if the landing is happening in a field near to the road, again be aware of other drivers who may suddenly do unpredictable manoeuvres in their panic. Quite often what appeared to be a very quiet country lane suddenly becomes one big traffic jam as everyone stops to watch the balloon land.

What is not desirable at this moment is for spectators to rush on to the landowners field without his permission. It doesn't foster good farmer relations if his first sight of the balloon is with a large number of people tramping around on his land. The balloonists are obviously to blame in his eyes. It is therefore most useful if at least one crew member can be stationed to stop people from trespassing whilst the pilot can decided with the remaining crew the best way to contact the farmer.

What can be done if the balloon is lost and the retrieve crew is not in radio communication? Hopefully, before take-off, the pilot will have given the retrieve crew a telephone number. This should be a telephone which will be manned during the time of flying and subsequent retrieve. If the crew do not turn up soon after landing the pilot will seek a telephone, call this number and leave a message as to his whereabouts, probably including a map reference and any information which will assist the retrieve crew in locating him. The retrieve, having allowed time for the pilot to call in, can then make their call and receive his message. Both sides must remember to carry phonecards and change for call boxes unless either, or both, have the luxury of portable or car phones. (NB. it is illegal to operate a portable phone while airborne.) Answerphones with remote message receivers can also be used for retrieve and do not entail a third party having to remain by the phone.

Sometimes the retrieve crew can be sure that the balloon has landed in a definite area, but they cannot decide on, or locate the most suitable access to the spot. In a case like this the pilot may well walk to the nearest road and hope that the crew will drive past. A flight cylinder, or something else instantly recognisable, may be left in a gateway as a 'clue' to the balloon's whereabouts.

Fig. 22–2   Packing up

If a landing has been made just before dusk, the retrieve could well be searching for the balloon in the dark. Even if the envelope has been deflated the pilot may still be able to use the burner as a guide for the crew.

The retrieve vehicle should never be driven on to private property without the owner's permission. Always carry the equipment out of the field to the vehicle if permission cannot be obtained. If the ground crew has to pass the farm house to get to where the balloon has landed it can save time if they contact the farmer for permission to retrieve the balloon.

Landowner relations is a subject which should be uppermost in all balloonists minds. Retrieve crew members, especially newcomers to the countryside, need to be aware of the country code. Not all the points of which are covered in the BBAC: Pilot Code of Conduct. Crew on the ground should also take the following into account:-

- dogs kept under control if let out of the retrieve vehicle.
- footpaths kept to wherever possible, rather than walking through crop.
- gates and stiles taken to cross hedges, fences and walls. Livestock could escape if field boundaries are damaged by persons climbing over or through them.
- gates should always be left as they were found (open or closed).
- litter taken home.
- no unnecessary noise. Livestock can be just as disturbed by noisy traffic and people as they can be by balloons.

Occasionally, for a number of reasons, the landing field may not be suitable for the balloon to be laid down and dismantled. There may be a power line across the field, it may have crop, it may be just too small or even too muddy. For whatever reason, the pilot may wish the crew to guide the still inflated balloon nearer to a gateway, or over the field boundary, hedge or fence. Perhaps into a more suitable field to one side of the flight path, or even on to a wide grassy roadside verge. This is known as a 'walk-out'.

Every balloonist has his or her own special way of packing away their envelope, dismantling the burner and basket etc. However in most cases it seems that P1, having rendered the burner system safe, will attempt to get out of any actual physical work by either hastening off to find the land-owner or doing what is referred to as 'PR work', but which appears to be just chatting, among the spectators. In either case it will be expected that the crew will have practically finished packing up before he rejoins them! There are a couple of tricks the crew can retaliate with, but it rather depends on whether they wish to crew for the pilot again . . . .

In the first case they can prevent this happening by not turning up on the scene until P1 has had ample time to get everything packed up. He's not to know that his crew are parked along the road, hidden by a thick hedge waiting for all the hard work to be done.

The other way is to socialise among themselves, perhaps start on the hot coffee, until P1 has finished chatting and is ready to personally supervise the packing up.

Having got the equipment packed and the landowner thanked, all that is left to be done is the return trip home and the refuelling — generally the crew first and the tanks last! Any crew who helps with the refuelling of cylinders must be aware of the procedures necessary for handling propane.

In competition flying the balloon pilot needs a well practised retrieve crew who can find him speedily and without fuss, since the time to complete a task is usually limited. Crew too need to be conversant with the competition rules as they can inadvertently incur penalty points for their pilot if they infringe some clauses. Competition tasks are often flown in faster conditions than a pilot would choose to fly in for fun and retrieving in these conditions, usually in an unknown area, can be an exciting challenge, providing the crew can survive a week or weekend of very early mornings, late nights, little food and hard physical labour!

Believe it or not, crew members do this time and again, even giving up precious annual holiday time for the privilege. Once ballooning gets into your system there is very little hope of leading a 'normal' life again!

23

OBSERVING

The BBAC Competitions Club organises competitive ballooning in the UK. There are weekend Grand Prix competitions throughout the year and an annual week long British National Championships.

To record task details and to see 'fair play' each competing pilot nominates an observer for the observer pool who comes under the control of the Chief Observer.

Almost any experienced crew person can be nominated as an observer, providing they do not exceed the maximum weight limit. Observing in competitions also provides an excellent opportunity for meeting other crews and pilots and possibly the chance of a balloon flight. Persons not attached to a balloon team can still participate as an observer for a competition meet, by applying direct to the Chief Observer.

An observer needs an impartial approach towards the competitors but it does not have to be an unfriendly one. An observer is just that, someone who observes, without having to interpret rules or stand in judgement of a competitor.

Eligibility
Competition rules state that an observer's weight must not be more than 80 kg (12 stone 9 pounds) fully dressed — including flying clothes, boots and crash helmet!

An observer should be willing to fly in the basket if invited.

Map reading ability, as well as a good understanding of both the Ordnance Survey 1:50,000 scale maps and 1:500,000 scale (half million) aeronautical charts, are necessary skills.

Duties
An observer must be familiar with the competition rules. Usually a competitor will receive a copy for his observer in advance of a competition.

Observers must attend the preliminary observers' briefing which will usually include a training session for newcomers, and all task briefings where they will be allocated to a different pilot for each flight. Also at task briefing they will receive a copy of the task details for that flight and an observer report sheet. (Instruction on how to complete report sheets is usually included in any preliminary briefing.)

After task briefing observers go with their allocated pilot and crew to the launch site and prepare to record the various times and details requested on their report sheets. They can offer to help with inflation. Some crews will be very pleased to have an extra pair of hands, but it should be realised that inflation in competition conditions is not the leisurely social occasion it can be in other circumstances. Some crews may work to a very strict routine to ensure nothing is forgotten or omitted and additional help could be a hindrance. In this case do not be offended when an offer of help is turned down.

If not invited to fly with the pilot the observer will follow on retrieve with the crew. Observers are not permitted to drive the retrieve vehicle but should be allocated a window seat to enable them to keep the observed balloon and others in sight where possible. Map reading help may be given if asked for by the crew. However, it is at their own risk and not the observer's responsibility if the balloon is lost!

Measurement of marker positions is another duty of an observer, together with the recording of dropping times if the marker is seen at this point. An observer may be asked to note details or information by a competitor during a task. Any flying incidents or infringements should also be noted concerning other competitors.

Observers are not allowed to advise competitors on any interpretation of the rules nor may they handle the balloon controls during a competition flight other than at the final landing with the pilot's permission and direction.

On return to Competition Control observers report for debriefing on their completed report sheets.

An observer should also help the pilot and crew in dealings with farmers or landowners.

Basic equipment
Normal crewing/flying wear and sensible footwear suited to weather and time of year is generally all the clothing required.

Equipment needed:-

watch and/or stopwatch	— digital can be easier to use since figures are clearly shown
gloves	— need to be hardwearing
pen & pencil	— together with eraser, pencil sharpener and spares too, since they can easily get lost or mislaid.
felt tip pens	— for marking up additional PCZ's
protractor	— a square one can be easier to use on maps
compass	— for taking and checking bearings
clipboard	— a great help for writing and organising paperwork
spray paint	— a small can, used to record marker positions in some instances
binoculars	— useful, but not an absolute necessity
torch	— for marker location in the dark!
helmet	— even if not worn normally, bear in mind that competition flying may be done in faster conditions than an observer is used to and a helmet is a very sensible safety precaution.
small holdall or rucksack	— to contain everything

Anyone familiar with the nature of ballooning will know that meals can sometimes be very few and far between so, if space permits, a small emergency food supply can be a godsend (fruit, chocolate, carton of fruit juice, etc.). Of course some crews may invite their observer to share their 'goodies', but not all come well supplied!

Non-essential equipment, but items which make observing an easier task could include an Airtour Ballooning Calculator (see Chapter 6: Ballooning Equipment). This simplifies and speeds up the task of marking up observers' maps. Another useful item is an Airtour Observer Organiser; a padded 3-fold document case, it comes complete with A4 clipboard to hold task sheets, observer report sheets, etc.; clear pockets for maps, pockets for notebook, ballooning calculator; elastic loops for pen/pencils and HBM scale/ruler; pencil case and attachment for stopwatch or compass. When in use the clipboard fits in an external pocket so the case can be closed to protect the other contents.

Observers are not encouraged to spend their time taking photographs since this will detract from their participation in the task in hand. Certainly an observer may not take a camera in the basket or take photos from the air without the pilot's permission. If the observer is a keen photographer and cannot travel without a camera it is preferable to carry a small compact camera. A pilot is more likely to agree to a pocket-sized camera on board rather than a huge bag of cameras, lenses, tripod etc!

Maps
The **Ordnance Survey** maps (1:50,000) have a scale of 2 cm to 1 km and are conveniently marked with a grid of 2 cm squares which can be a great help when estimating distances. An observer must be familiar with the symbols which represent different features since these features may be used as reference for the location of markers.

The ability to use map references is essential and is covered in the **Navigation** chapter in Section 4 of this manual. It is not a difficult task and can be made easier and more accurate by use of a 'roamer'. This is a right angled scale marked in tenths of a 2 cm square which shows the third figure of eastings and northings and allows for a fourth figure to be estimated. A Ballooning Calculator includes a roamer for this purpose.

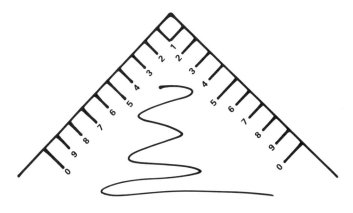

Fig. 23–1   A roamer

Just as accurate, but not as easy to use to get a third figure, is a ruler marked in millimetres. Remember that 2 mm is equal to one tenth of a grid square.

Before a contest maps need to be marked up to show the locations of the prohibited competition zones — **PCZ's**. These are areas where flying is restricted in some way. There may be no landings allowed or there may be a minimum height stated for overflying. Sensitive areas notified under the BBAC Pilot Code of Conduct and published in *Pilots Circular* will usually be included, along with any declared specifically for the duration of the competition. Identified by serial numbering new ones may be announced and given numbers at task briefings.

If flying during a task, the flight path of the balloon should be marked with small pencil crosses as it flies over easily identified features. When the marker is dropped a quick sketch should be made to show its proximity to hedges, trees, tracks etc. and the exact location marked on the map. If the marker cannot be found afterwards the pilot may be eligible for a score based on the observer's information.

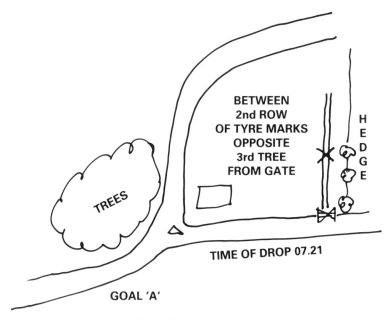

Fig. 23–2   Sketch of marker drop

Marker measurement

The method used depends on the proximity of the marker to the goal, and the type of task. If a task has meant that competitors are all aiming markers at one goal, officials may be there measuring marker distances from the target and all an observer will have to do is to confirm that the measurement has been taken and double check the distance if required.

Where a marker is close to a set target it is a simple task to measure the distance with a tape measure but if the target is one perhaps declared by the pilot, a centre point has to be determined first. Details for doing this are included in the Observers Handbook issued by the Competitions Club.

If a marker is a long way from a target it may still be possible to measure it using the tape and recording how many lengths of tape plus the final measurement, i.e. 4 x 30 m tape lengths + 2 metres. Brightly coloured golf tees can be useful for marking the end of the length of tape so the crew or whoever is helping knows where to start the next length measurement.

If the target or goal is nowhere in sight (a not infrequent occurrence!) an observer can decide to measure accurately the position of the marker in relation to two or more features which are shown on the map. The marker position can then be plotted by officials after debriefing and measurements taken from the map for scoring purposes. To ensure greater acccuracy the operations centre usually has a 1:25,000 chart (4 cm = 1 km) to measure from.

Sketch maps should always be drawn on the observer's report form showing the location of a marker and where measurements have been taken from to avoid any ambiguity at debriefing.

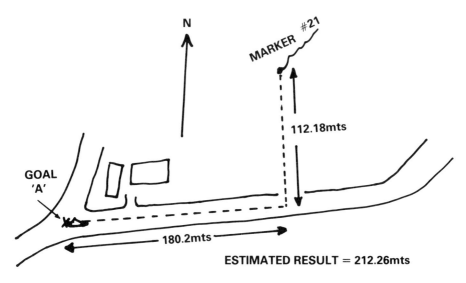

Fig. 23–3   Final sketch map

A lost marker can mean that a pilot has no score and is very disappointing for all concerned. Everyone is tempted to keep looking until it is found. Fortunately for the observer there is a time limit for a search and so they should not have to spend hours in deserted areas at midnight looking for that elusive marker!

On completion of a task but before debriefing, the pilot will sign the observer's report sheet to show that he/she is satisfied the information included is complete and correct.

Experience of observing can be useful for other duties at competition meets, such as debriefers who check through each observer's report sheet with them at the end of a task to ensure accurate scoring.

Accredited observer
Recognition as an accredited observer usually requires the successful completion of eight to ten competition tasks to the satisfaction of the competition officials.

This opens up the opportunity for observing in international ballooning competitions. Every year the BBAC is asked for accredited UK observers to attend the European or the World Hot Air Balloon Championships. These are held on alternate years and present an interesting way to visit other countries, although there is generally very little time for sight-seeing during the competition period itself.

24

MAINTENANCE

A carefully flown and well maintained balloon will generally have a much longer flying life than one which is frequently flown to the limits and allowed to deteriorate with few defects being rectified. Happily, most people value their lives sufficiently to take the time and effort to ensure that all their equipment is in good working order. The old saying 'a stitch in time . . .' can be very relevant to balloon repairs.

Having taken delivery of a beautiful new balloon the next most important consideration is where it is to be stored. Balloon fabrics and load tapes can be susceptible to mildew damage if stored damp for even a short time, so a dry area is a priority. However if everything is stored together it must also be remembered that propane and flight cylinders need to be stored in cool, well ventilated conditions. Baskets too need a well aired resting place. They are none the worse for getting wet occasionally but need to dry out well afterwards.

If everything is stored in a trailer bear in mind that damp and rain can collect in the bottom leaving equipment sitting in puddles. Also, few envelope bags are completely waterproof and water can seep through to the envelope on long trailer journeys in bad weather — rain seems able to penetrate the most unexpected spaces in trailers however well covered.

Envelope bags can also promise a cosy nesting place for mice so care should be taken if storage is to be in barns or other farm buildings!

Certificate of Airworthiness
There is often confusion as to what a Certificate of Airworthiness actually is. It is not the inspection report (Form IR4) stuck in the balloon log book each year by a BBAC inspector.

A certified balloon will have an actual certificate which together with the manufacturers manual/handbook forms the C of A.

When a new balloon is issued with a C of A, it means that the balloon complies with all the requirements set out in **CAP494: British Airworthiness Requirements — Part 31 Manned Free Balloons**.

These basically cover:

- Flight
  - weight limits
  - performance
  - controllability
- Strength
  - limit loads
  - safety factors
- Design and construction
  - materials
  - methods of fabrication
  - all systems
  - inspection

- Equipment   — function
                                            — installation
- Operating Limitations
  and information   — for continued airworthiness

The balloon manufacturer certifies that the balloon complies with all these requirements. It therefore follows that if anything on the balloon is modified, changed or replaced without approval from the manufacturer or by not using approved methods and tested materials then the Certificate of Airworthiness is invalid.

To maintain a C of A any repair or approved modification must be passed by a BBAC approved inspector. (Category 1, 2, 3 or — for fabric repairs only — category 5) and a copy of Form IR4 completed to this effect. The manufacturer's manual will give details on how permitted repairs should be carried out.

To renew a C of A the balloon has to be checked over by an inspector every twelve months or 100 hours whichever is the sooner. The inspector will then complete a Form IR4 and the relevant portion affixed in the balloon log.

For non-commercial flying a current Certificate of Airworthiness is not a legal requirement (although your insurance policy may require the balloon to have one). However an annual inspection of all equipment by a BBAC appointed inspector is a good idea for all balloons whether or not it is done for a C of A renewal. An inspector may be able to point out defects or potential trouble spots before they become too difficult or expensive to rectify. Prevention can be better than cure in many instances.

General maintenance
With the wide range of balloon envelopes, baskets and burners it is not possible to cover everything concerning their maintenance in this manual. For more detailed information the balloon manufacturer's handbook or manual should always be consulted.

Envelope care
If a wet envelope is left in its bag for more than a day or two it runs the risk of developing mildew or moulds on the fabric and load tapes. While this may not initially result in physical damage the cosmetic appearance of the balloon is often greatly affected, with black speckles or larger areas of white or rusty looking discolourations. (Colours can sometimes run in fabrics stored damp, as well). In some instances the p.u. coating may deteriorate, leading to envelope porosity. Re-inflating an envelope or flying again is a good way of drying it out, but it is important to realise that although the ripstop itself dries quite quickly, load tapes can take thirty minutes or more to do so. In some cases high temperatures to very wet lines and tapes can cause shrinking (along similar lines to the effect tumble-dryers have on some fabrics!).

Mud (and worse!) on light coloured fabrics obviously shows up more than on darker ones, but large-scale washing operations are not practical or advisable, and the only way of keeping an envelope really clean is not to take it out of the bag and fly it! However, flying in dry conditions and avoiding cow-pastures for landings is probably the next best way of retaining a presentable envelope.

Obviously most pilots carry out a comprehensive inspection of the envelope on their pre-flight checks, but some areas are not inspected as a matter of course and a check of these at regular intervals is good practice.

Flying wires should not show signs of fraying, or permanent kinks. Heat can cause discoloration of wires and repeated overheating can lead to them becoming stiff and brittle, with kinks which stay bent. Their junction with the load tapes at the mouth, concealed by protective 'muffs', is an area which can often be a victim of overheating. To check them, especially if the muff appears burnt or crisp, is simply a matter of drawing back the covering to reveal the join.

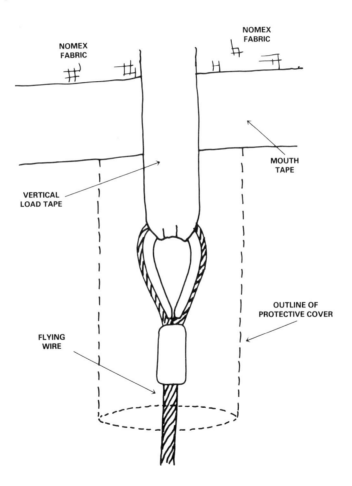

Fig. 24–1   Flying wire/load tape junction

Control lines need replacing if they show signs of damage, either frayed or melted areas, since these weakened places could fail during operation of the line, with embarrassing results.

Carabiners need to have free running screw-gates. A regular application of a silicon based lubricant will keep them in good condition. A bent or twisted carabiner should be replaced at once.

Envelope attachment points for control lines and parachute cords should be periodically checked for loose stitching or signs of wear, and pulleys inspected to ensure they are free from loose threads, grass etc. If a pulley seizes the heat generated by friction as a rope is pulled through can cause melting of the rope. If the balloon seems to develop an increased thirst for fuel with nothing else amiss, check that the parachute is sealing correctly. With a straightforward seal, the outline of the envelope edge should show as a well defined line around the parachute when the envelope is inflated and the tabs broken. If not, consult with the balloon manufacturer.

If a **heat-flag** drops out during flight it can easily be replaced. Following this the **temperature indicator label** should always be checked to see whether this also has recorded a high temperature. If so, the balloon manufacturer's instructions should be followed regarding further checks.

Velcro tabs on the parachute and the top edge of the envelope tend to collect grass seeds, loose threads etc. — especially the 'hooks' portion — which reduces their 'sticking power'. These should be cleaned occasionally using a wire suede brush. The exposed 'hooks' portion can sometimes raise a fuzziness on adjacent load tapes and to help prevent this some pilots reclose the tabs before packing the envelope away.

On many envelopes the free load tapes at the crown may be joined at one or more places by a circular **restraining tape**. Since this tape is sewn using a very small 'gate' of stitches it is advisable to inspect these at regular intervals to ensure the stitching is intact.

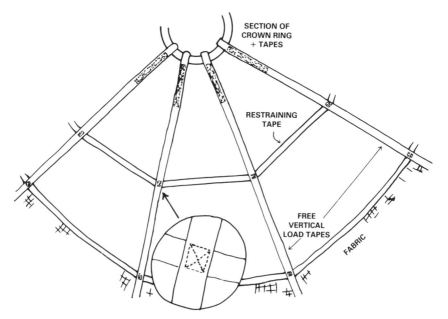

SECTION OF
CROWN RING
+ TAPES

RESTRAINING
TAPE

FREE
VERTICAL
LOAD TAPES

FABRIC

Fig. 24–2   Restraint web

Burns and tears

An envelope can be flown with a certain amount of damage, without invalidating its C of A, if the damage is below the level stipulated in the handbook, and providing only the ripstop nylon or Nomex is involved. If there is any damage to load tapes or wires this is not the case. Fabric repairs in this area can be made by any recognised method, i.e. sewing, glued patches or self-adhesive ripstop tape.

Damage above this line renders the balloon unairworthy and needs to be repaired before flight using approved methods. Any repair here will need to be examined and approved by a BBAC appointed inspector before reinstatement of the C of A.

Sewn repairs can involve whole or part panel replacement or patches. These should be done in accordance with manufacturers' guidelines. If load tapes need to be unpicked and resewn it will probably be outside the scope of a domestic sewing machine.

Basket

It is surprising just how much mud can collect in the **basket** on some landings! Left, it can pack into the weave, harbouring moisture and if this happens in the area round the base covered by hide, it can lead to deterioration of the cane/willow because the moisture cannot dry out. Prevent this by giving the basket a good clean with a stiff brush as part of the regular maintenance routine.

An occasional hosing down with water on the outside will not do any harm either, providing the basket has a chance to dry before being packed away. This can be an opportunity to straighten a mis-shapen basket if it can be held in a good position until dry.

Suede tops can be brushed with a suede brush to clean off mud and scuffs and leather tops will benefit from a good buff with shoe polish.

The burner system

Burners should be kept clean of soot which can build up on coils, and a visual check made regularly on the swivel mountings to make sure locking devices are in position. If the jets are of the screw-in type check regularly that they have not worked loose. They do not generally do this in flight, but it can happen in transit.

Hoses should be visually checked for damage. A damp cloth can be used to clean off mud. Again they are more likely to be damaged in transit than in the air, possibly as a result of being trapped under cylinders or other pieces of equipment in the vehicle or trailer. It is important to keep **connectors** clean and free from grit. Small pouches to put on as soon as they are disconnected from cylinders are a good idea.

Flight cylinders

Cylinders do not require a great deal of maintenance. They need an occasional examination for external damage, valve connections need to be kept clean and grit free, and o-rings or seals need to be regularly checked for signs of damage.

Some connectors are fitted with plastic caps which protect o-rings and seals when not in use. (A visit to the local hardware or DIY store can sometimes come up with caps of suitable size if none are fitted.) Since seals are not a costly item, some pilots consider it practical to change them at an annual inspection rather than wait for a problem to occur. Connectors can benefit from an occasional spray with a silicon based lubricant. Sticking valves, faulty fuel gauges or leaks generally need investigating by the manufacturer or repair station. The suspect cylinder should be emptied by careful venting. (See Chapter 27: Propane Handling.)

Care should be taken with cylinders in transit. They should always travel upright and firmly secured.

25

GENERAL SAFETY

The saying 'safety is no accident' is very true, but it can also be said that safety is basically the application of simple common sense.

Unfortunately, accidents do sometimes happen and then there are definite reporting procedures to follow, laid down by air law. The CAA defines a reportable accident as one in which there is fatal or serious injury, or where the aircraft suffers damage requiring major repair. (See Chapter 28: Air Law.)

Minor accidents which do not come under the above definition are referred to as 'incidents'. The BBAC Flying and Technical committees, through the BBAC Safety Officer are interested in all ballooning incidents. Their definition of an incident is; any occurrence or fault which causes damage to balloon, person or object, or which in the opinion of the reporter, might have done.'

There is no need to supply any names when submitting a report. The balloon registration and the signature of the person submitting the report (not necessarily the person involved in the incident) are all that is required.

Incident reporting serves to highlight actual or potential material, component or design failures in balloons and also possible short-comings in pilot training. The BBAC can then take appropriate action where necessary to avoid similar incidents.

Shared knowledge that will help to maintain the good safety record of ballooning must be beneficial to all balloonists, so do not be reluctant or embarrassed to submit a report on any incident.

BBAC SAFETY CODE

These 'Golden Rules' have been adopted as the BBAC Safety Code, following extensive discussion at instructor weekends, and the analysis of incident report forms. They are intended as guidelines only and are obviously not a definitive or exclusive summary of ballooning safety. It is hoped, however, that they will provide a useful reference for pilots, trainee pilots and crew.

1 A balloon must always be restrained during inflation

The advantages of this far outweigh any disadvantages. There should be a short (say 5m) restraint line for this purpose.

Restraint means that a pilot always knows that he has the balloon under control, no matter what the weather, or his crew, decide to do. There should be no exception to restraining, even on what looks like a calm day. Gusts may arrive at any time, even on the stillest summer evening.

2 Capable of flight when prepared for flight

Before the balloon is upright, everything practical should be done that would be necessary for flight **even if the initial intention is not to free fly**. After the balloon is upright, pre-flight checks should be carried out. Apart from the possibility of breaking free it is in the nature of ballooning for people to make sudden changes of mind about their intentions, perhaps because the weather changes.

3 Hold blast valve when burning

If you need to turn it off, then it's a lot quicker if your hand's already there.

4 Leave burner totally safe

When a pilot moves away from the burner, either during inflation or after landing, there should be no fuel in either the main burner hoses or the pilot light hose(s).

5 No burning on touchdown

The main burner should always be **OFF** at the moment of touchdown, no matter how slow the flight, or soft the landing. Also, blast valves should not be held during touchdown, as this creates a risk of accidental use.

6 Gloves and headgear

Suitable gloves should be worn during inflation and be available in flight. Protective headgear or helmets should be available for use when necessary. Be aware of the recommendations in your flight manual regarding gloves and headgear, as you may be flying outside the terms of your C of A if these are not available.

7 Lead with liquid and light last

When carrying out a burner test, or immediately prior to hot inflation, open one tank valve and check for leaks; turn on pilot valve at cylinder (and burner) then light the pilot light. This way a large leak upstream of the blast valve is not given an ignition source.

8 Extinguishers available

In addition to one fire extinguisher that should always be carried in the basket, a second should be positioned near the fan during inflation. A crew member should be responsible for this and briefed accordingly.

9 One pole leads to another

When making an approach or landing, do not continue the approach if only one electricity/telephone pole can be seen.

10 Down and out

Do not exceed 500 fpm downwards below 500 ft agl. When doing a cold descent the roundout should be started in good time so as to achieve this.

11 Turn off first
In the event of fire, attempt to isolate the source of the propane first, by turning off the appropriate valve.

12 One turn is on
For tank liquid feed valves that are actuated by wheels, one full turn away from shut is full on. This means that only one turn is required to turn off.

13 No sparks
All electrical equipment should be off during inflation. This includes radios, which may generate sparks in the receive mode. When refuelling, remove all likely sources of ignition from the basket/cylinder jackets.

14 Minimum propane at all times
During inflation and flight there should be the minimum propane admitted to the system from the tanks. During inflation only one side of the burner system should be live, until the balloon is upright. If a manifolding system is used, when in flight only one tank on each side of the burner should be live.

★   ★   ★   ★

FIRE EXTINGUISHERS
To burn, a flame needs a continuing supply of oxygen. Deprived of this a flame is extinguished. To deprive a fire of oxygen is therefore the aim of a fire extinguisher. Since the seat of a fire is usually unapproachable an extinguisher must also be capable of reaching the fire when operated from some distance away.

Water, powder, gases, and chemical foam can all have the desired effect of smothering flames and therefore depriving them of oxygen. Which one to use will depend on the source of the fire. (Water, for example, should not be used on liquid or fuel fires since it could spread the burning liquid further or on electrical fires where it could electrocute the operator.)

Whatever the cause of fire an extinguisher should always be directed at the base of the flames.

There is a recognised code which indicates the suitability of an extinguisher for various categories of fire.

paper, wood, textiles

inflammable gases/liquids

live electrical equipment

Some types of extinguisher can be recharged after use, whereas others simply need replacing. Some enable you to check for serviceability by carrying a pressure gauge usually marked with a green (OK) sector and a red (replace) sector. Others may have a pressure 'disc' which need replacing if the disc can be pressed in, or need weighing to check that they are still fully primed.

Operation differs from extinguisher to extinguisher and instructions for use are clearly marked on each type.

Perhaps the two types most suitable for ballooning are BCF (Halon) and Dry Chemical.

BCF (Halon)

This extinguisher contains Halon 1211 (Bromo-Chlorodi-Fluoromethane) in a liquid gas form. It is released as a spray and is capable of arresting most types of fire. It leaves no residue which can be an advantage over other kinds of extinguisher.

Dry Chemical

This type contains a dry powder with carbon dioxide. Again it is suitable for most types of fire but has the disadvantage of leaving a powder residue which is corrosive to aluminium alloys. Thorough cleaning is extremely important after use, especially if instruments and flight cylinders have been involved.

The ideal extinguisher to fit into the balloon basket will probably be selected for compactness and light weight. It will need to be carefully mounted so that it is readily accessible but also protected to avoid personal injury on landings.

FIRST AID

As the name implies, first aid is just that, the initial treatment a casualty receives at the scene of an accident. It is this care which can save life, prevent the worsening of injuries or other conditions and be a step towards recovery.

A knowledge of first aid can be useful for everyone but more so perhaps for balloonists who often find themselves in remote areas without ready access to medical aid. Not everyone has the time or inclination to undertake a first aid course leading to a First Aider's certificate awarded by one of the Voluntary First Aid Associations, (St John Ambulance, The British Red Cross Society or St Andrew's Ambulance Association), but an understanding of the major first aid techniques and basic principles could be a great help in an emergency.

The Voluntary First Aid Associations have produced a joint publication the 'First Aid Manual' which deals with first aid in an easily understandable style, and could be a useful addition to the balloon equipment.

It is good practice to carry some form of first aid kit in the basket. It does not have to be a cumbersome commercial kit — just a few basics such as a plastic bottle of water, cottonwool, medicated wipes, an elastic bandage and a few plasters, could cope with most of the more minor injuries likely to be encountered.

Apart from cuts and grazes, another possible injury to be treated could be a burn. Burns need cooling as quickly as possible, the best method being under a running tap — not often available when ballooning. If a bottle of water is not to hand, any cold liquid i.e. coke or lemonade would serve in an emergency. If clothing has adhered to the burn area do not attempt to remove it as this could cause further damage. All burns should be covered to protect from infection, but no creams or lotions should be applied.

SECTION 4
THEORY FOR PPLs

26

AIRMANSHIP

Airmanship is defined as 'the practical application of training, skill, experience and professional judgement'. It is a pilot's behaviour and attitude when flying, with regard to rules and regulations affecting the flight, other air users and the people in his care.

A pilot must show due regard for air law, with special reference to the height/altitude of the balloon when flying over built-up areas, hazards, restricted airspace, people or vessels.

Other factors affecting the height of the balloon which also need to be taken into account are those agreed in the BBAC: Pilot's Code of Conduct, when overflying stock or specially notified sensitive areas. The use of a silent burner, should be demonstrated when flying in the vicinity of livestock. It is worth noting that it is not only the livestock on the flight path which can be frightened by the approach of a balloon, but also those animals off to one side or the other. Animals can also be frightened if they are confined in buildings and often with very damaging results. Barnes, sheds, chickenhouses should be treated as containing livestock to be on the safe side. If animals appear to have been disturbed it is advisable to return after the flight to check that none have suffered as a result.

It is a courtesy, when planning to fly in an unknown area, to contact the local LRO. At balloon meets, the organisers will have done so on behalf of visiting pilots who should ensure that their maps carry all the current sensitive areas.

Knowledge of the BBAC: Pilot Code of Conduct also has to be demonstrated in flight, in the choice of landing site and post landing procedures.

Whilst keeping a careful watch over the land being covered during flight a pilot must also keep a look out in the air for other aircraft and changes in the weather conditions. When flying in company with other balloons a pilot must maintain an awareness of their position in relation to his own especially those passing out of sight above, or flying below. Generally speaking the balloon above should give way to one below, but the pilot of the one below should also bear in mind the time lag between burning and a balloon climbing. A balloon making a rapid ascent could climb up into one above before the upper one had time to build up a compatible climb rate. It is therefore in the interests of both pilots to maintain sufficient separation to avoid this. The use of an air horn can tell a pilot that there is a balloon, out of his sight, above him. In this situation, the pilot in the lower balloon should react by decreasing his rate of climb by any means available.

Weather conditions can sometimes change quite dramatically for the worse after take-off and an awareness of what is happening is essential if a safe landing is to be accomplished. After a calm take-off it is not uncommon to find that the speed of the wind increases. Careful monitoring of the flight speed is therefore a sensible exercise to repeat at intervals. It should be noted that the type of terrain being flown over can influence the windspeed and that the sea-breeze effect early in an evening can have a far reaching consequence inland. A flight on a warm day can encounter thermal effects with unpredictable changes in direction and height. A sign that heat is beginning to produce these effects is the build up of small white fluffy cumulus clouds.

Occasionally a bank of rain cloud will move quicker in the upper wind currents and overtake the balloon. Flying in rain is not a comfortable experience. The envelope becomes heavier and more difficult to handle as the fabric soaks up the moisture. The excess rain flows down the load tapes to the flying wires and so into the basket. Puddles form in the top of the parachute and leakage through the seams can shower down directly on to the pilot light, with embarrassing results. A wet envelope should be dried as soon as possible to avoid damage from mildew or moulds.

Proper care for the safety and well being of passengers during flight is an important aspect of airmanship. This starts before the flight with the pre-flight briefing, so passengers know what to expect. Passengers, in their excitement or apprehension, often forget what they have been told so a pilot may need to repeat instructions once they are airborne. A pilot should always warn his passengers when an approach is being made so they have time to prepare for landing. Ensure that helmets, if carried, are worn when landing.

After a flight, having contacted the landowner and packed away, the last remaining demonstration of airmanship must be crew refreshment in some form or other, depending on time of day!

Good airmanship really boils down to simple common sense, and consideration for others.

27

PROPANE HANDLING

Propane (C_3H_8) is a Liquefied Petroleum Gas (L.P.G.). It is marketed commercially as a domestic and industrial fuel in pressure cylinders or in bulk quantities to static pressure tanks. Readily flammable when mixed with air in the right proportions it is this property which makes it suitable as a fuel for ballooning.

Propane as a liquid is colourless, but on contact with air it will be visible as a white spray. The boiling point is approximately $-40°$ centigrade and if temperatures are higher, the liquid form will rapidly evaporate by boiling off, unless the pressure acting on the liquid is increased. Propane in liquid form is therefore stored in pressure containers (i.e. fuel cylinders). Pressure in such containers will vary with the ambient temperature — a rise in temperature causes evaporation, which increases the internal pressure until pressure/temperature equilibrium is reached; and a fall in temperature causes condensation, which decreases the internal pressure until again equilibrium is reached.

One litre of propane weighs 500g or 1.1 lb approx.

On a cold day it should be noted that pressure in a cylinder will be significantly reduced and that this will have a derogatory effect on burner performance. An easy and very efficient way of increasing pressure in a cylinder is to pour hot water over the cylinder to raise its temperature by a few degrees. Placing a cover around the cylinder will ensure that the remedy will remain effective for some time. Some balloonists prefer to pressurize their cylinders with nitrogen. This occupies the vapour space in the cylinder and so this remedy cannot be used in a master cylinder where propane vapour is used to run the pilot light. **Never use a naked flame to heat a cylinder**.

In the liquid phase, propane has a relatively high co-efficient of expansion. Therefore, a cylinder is not completely filled with liquid but 'ullage' or free space is left to permit liquid expansion within normal variations in temperature without overstressing the cylinder. The ullage space contains propane in its vapour phase.

To facilitate the early detection of leaks, normally odour free propane has a distinctive stench added. Leakage can also produce a hissing sound and/or cause freezing. The appearance of 'frost' on pipework or connections should be investigated. Obviously, never search for a leak with a naked flame. Soapy water will produce a gathering of foam when brushed over a leak.

At ambient temperature the gas is one and a half times heavier than air which means that leaking vapour will not readily disperse at ground level, and a build up could lead to the risk of explosion. (Hence the need to be sure to keep cigarette and pipe smokers away from cylinders.) Vapour can

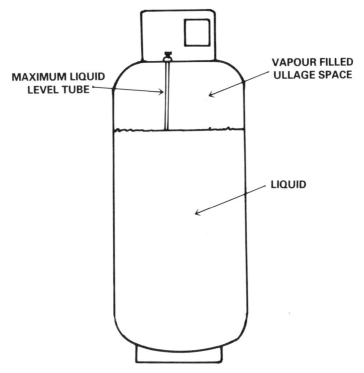

MAXIMUM LIQUID
LEVEL TUBE

VAPOUR FILLED
ULLAGE SPACE

LIQUID

Fig. 27–1   A 'full' cylinder showing ullage space

also flow downhill like a liquid, forming puddles in low lying areas which can take a long time to disperse. The gas is flammable at a mix with air of between 2%–10% approximately, so it doesn't need a lot to achieve an explosive mixture in these conditions. For this reason refuelling or venting fuel near drains should be avoided at all costs.

FLIGHT CYLINDERS
The types of cylinder in common use for ballooning are manufactured from aluminium or stainless steel, in several sizes. They are all fitted with a **safety relief valve** above the vapour space so that if undue high temperatures are brought to bear the resulting increase in internal pressure releases the valve until a safe internal pressure is achieved.

Extending down inside the cylinder, from a small **screw vent valve**, is a short dip tube. When filling a cylinder the vent valve should be opened to allow an audible escape of vapour. As soon as liquid is seen to emerge from it the supply should be turned off and the vent valve closed. This ensures that the necessary vapour space (ullage) is left at the top of the cylinder. With no vapour space the liquid could build up pressure sufficient to rupture the cylinder, or at least to release the safety relief valve. Therefore if overfilling occurs or is suspected the vent valve should be opened until emerging liquid gives way to vapour.

A **contents gauge** is fitted in the top of a cylinder. This generally gives a reading in percentage of contents remaining, with the first reading at 35%.

When the **liquid take-off valve** is opened the pressure in the cylinder forces liquid propane up through the **dip tube** and into a main burner hose. When the **vapour valve** is opened the pressure forces vapour through the pilot light hose. This pressure would be too high to operate the pilot light and therefore a regulator to reduce pressure is incorporated after the valve.

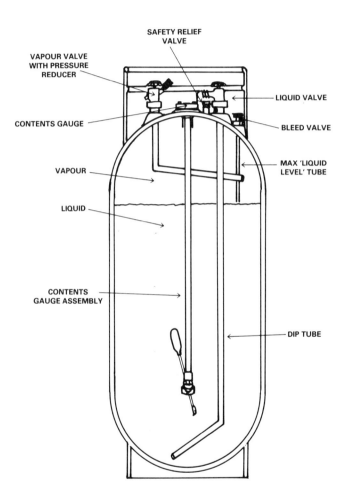

SAFETY RELIEF VALVE

VAPOUR VALVE WITH PRESSURE REDUCER

CONTENTS GAUGE

VAPOUR

LIQUID

CONTENTS GAUGE ASSEMBLY

LIQUID VALVE

BLEED VALVE

MAX 'LIQUID LEVEL' TUBE

DIP TUBE

Fig. 27–2   Cross-section of flight cylinder

Each cylinder has a guard around the top to protect valves from damage, but which allows for hose connection. There is also a protective rim to guard against external damage to the base. Even so, a cylinder should never be dragged along the ground. A roughened base rim could damage the floor of a basket in the long term.

REFUELLING

Since you are dealing with a potentially dangerous substance the greatest care should be taken at all times. 'No Smoking' signs should be prominently displayed and a fire extinguisher readily accessible. Skin contact with liquid propane can result in severe cold burns so it is always advisable to wear gloves when handling cylinders or refuelling. Contact with eyes should be avoided at all costs as should inhalation of the vapour.

The fewer people involved in the refuelling exercise the better from a safety point of view, and vehicles should be parked at a safe distance from the supply area, with engines switched off. Spectators should retire to a safe distance upwind of the site.

The supply area should be open to allow for easy dispersal of any vapour and not close to drains or any sources of ignition.

Balloon baskets although apparently of open weave can contain a build-up of vapour during refuelling when vapour is being vented, especially when also sited in a trailer. This is potentially a very dangerous situation and one to be avoided. Cylinders should always be removed from the basket for refuelling, and placed on open ground. If this is not possible an earthing clip must be used and no-one should remain in or near the basket during the exercise.

Flight cylinders can be refuelled by several means. 47 kg portable cylinder, static tank — with or without pump, autogas, or bulk tanker (common at balloon meets).

Where there are no means of pumping the propane from supply to cylinder there must be a differential in pressure to get a flow. The flow will be from the higher pressure to the lower one. Therefore if the supply is

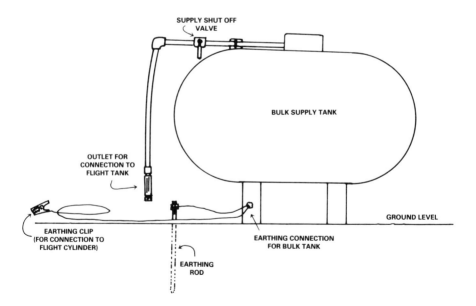

Fig. 27–3   A bulk tank

warmer than the flight cylinder, it will have a higher internal pressure and the fuel will flow in the desired direction. Warm water poured over the outside of the supply tank will increase the internal pressure sufficiently to get fuel flowing.

A refuelling hose is needed to connect from the flight cylinder to the supply. Couplings vary but a hose is needed which matches your cylinder connections and the supply generally used. Adaptors can be obtained if more than one type of connector is needed. When not in use the hoses should be stored carefully to keep connectors clean and free from damage.

To avoid the danger of static sparks when connecting or disconnecting cylinders it is sensible to have the supply earthed and bonded to the cylinder to be refuelled. The earthing clip should always be the first connection made before commencing and the last to be removed on completion of refuelling.

To refuel:
- connect earth clip to flight cylinder
- check that valves on flight tank and supply tank are in the 'off' position, connect refuelling hose.
- Once the connections are made open the flight tank valve and check the connections for leaks.
- If all is well, open the supply tank valve, followed by the bleed valve.
- Refuelling should stop at the first sign of liquid passing through the bleed valve.
- Close down the flight tank valve.
- Close the bleed valve.
- Close the supply valve.
- Remove hose from flight tank.
- Disconnect earth clip if used.

When refuelling is complete all hoses which contain liquid propane should be bled by depressing the self sealing valve found in the centre of the connector.

The cylinder connection valve should also be bled. Never use fingers to do this and always point valve away from the face, body and other people.

In an emergency situation always turn off the supply valve first, if at all possible.

As a general practice only refuel one cylinder at a time, keeping other cylinders at a safe distance. Then, in an emergency there is only the one to cope with.

The 47 kg domestic propane cylinders — commonly known as 'reds' or '104's' are generally obtained with just a vapour take-off. To get liquid propane out of these they need to be inverted to submerge the outlet in liquid propane. Care should be taken to keep the tank off vertical because there may be impurities collected in the base of the liquid propane and total inversion will allow these to flow into a flight cylinder. If the tank is allowed to tilt slightly then these impurities will collect in the 'shoulder' of the cylinder.

Less commonly available, there is a type of 47 kg cylinder with a liquid take-off and with these refuelling can be done from an upright position. They do, however, contain a safety valve which cuts off the flow of liquid if it exceeds a certain level and warming the tank with hot water to get a differential in pressures can activate this device if done too quickly. As the tank cools the flow will resume.

Static tank supply is generally a quicker process, more so if a pump is fitted. Pumps can be hand or electrically operated. The connecting procedure is the same as for other types of supply. There should be an earthing device to avoid static sparks, which could provide the means of ignition to a build-up of leaked vapour.

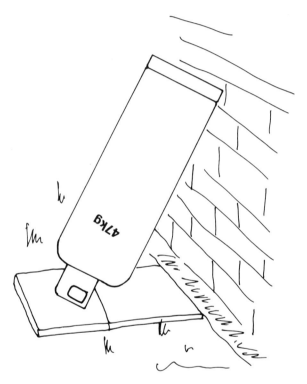

Fig. 27–4   A 47 kg tank inverted and 'tilted' prior to refuelling

At an auto gas supply, refuelling can be done as you would a gas driven vehicle, providing you have the correct hose connections.

At many balloon meets gas is provided by a tanker and generally the refuelling is done for you by the operator. Several cylinders can safely be refilled at one time making refuelling a quick and simple task.

EMERGENCY PROCEDURES

It is advisable to have a fire extinguisher to hand in the supply area. Preferably of the dry powder or BCF type. However the first consideration in the case of fire should be to shut down the supply of propane. If this is not possible then the extinguisher should be used to eliminate flames and the supply valve closed. However, if fire arises from a leak of propane which is not threatening anything else it is safer to allow the flame to burn rather than having leaking vapour which could reach an explosive mix with air. Bear in mind that as a cylinder becomes over heated the pressure relief valve could release creating long jets of flame. As the pressure is relieved the valve will reseal, but if heat is still being applied the vent is likely to open again.

Exposure to excessive heat from fire could cause a cylinder or tank to burst. Therefore if water can be played upon the cylinder for cooling, or the source of flame removed the danger can be averted.

If a cylinder develops a leak which cannot be closed off, most likely from a valve, it should be removed to wide open ground well away from all possible hazards and allowed to vent propane until empty, when the source of the leak can be inspected. It may be necessary to put up warning notices to alert others to the danger. In the case of leakage from a 47 kg tank, isolate as above and ask the dealer to collect it.

STORAGE OF CYLINDERS
(Both 47 kg and flight cylinders)
Many people store cylinders in garages, but ideally cylinders should always be stored in the open, away from drains or other places where a build up of vapour could create a hazard.

They should also be stored away from:
● direct heat — including full sunlight.
● naked flames — such as pilot lights on other gas appliances.
● sparks — from electrical appliances such as freezers, fridges.
● other combustible materials — petrol and paraffin.
  It is not advisable to store more than four cylinders in one area.

HANDLING AND TRANSPORT OF CYLINDERS
Cylinders should never be dropped or handled roughly. This could damage dip tubes or couplings. Couplings should be kept clean and treated occasionally with a silicone based lubricant. Never roll or drag cylinders.

Care is usually taken to ensure that cylinders are securely strapped into position in the balloon basket, but fewer balloonists take such care when transporting them in the retrieve vehicle or trailer. All cylinders, full or empty, should be secured for transit and should always travel upright. If in an enclosed trailer there should be air vents at floor level to avoid a build up of trapped vapour.

It is also good practice to display 'no-smoking' stickers where cylinders are stored and on trailers or retrieve vehicles.

28

AIR LAW

All aircraft wherever they are flying, have to conform to certain rules of the air in order to make aviation a safe pursuit for all participants. These rules, with slight variations from country to country, apply throughout the world.

The **International Civil Aviation Organisation** (ICAO), of which the United Kingdon is an active member, is the organisation with the aims of standardising aviation rules and procedures worldwide.

The **Civil Aviation Authority** (CAA) is the body responsible for civil aviation in the UK.

The basis of aviation law is the **Air Navigation Order** (ANO), supported by other legislations:–

> Rules of the Air and Air Traffic Control Regulations
> Air Navigation (General) Regulations
> Civil Aviation (Investigation of Accidents) Regulations
> UK Aeronautical Information Publication (UK AIP)

The CAA publishes a guide to Aviation Law, **CAP 85 — A guide to aviation law, flight rules and procedures for the Private Pilot's Licence**, which contains extracts from the above documents relevant to the private pilot and the PPL air law examination. It comes in loose-leaf binder form with the facility for updating as amendments are published. (The syllabus for the examination can be found in the CAA publication CAP 53 — The Student Pilots and Private Pilots Licence.) Many sections do not relate directly to ballooning, but a pilot does need to be aware of rules and regulations as they apply to other air users.

Whilst this manual sets out to clarify some of the points which relate more specifically to ballooning, a good working knowledge of CAP 85 is essential for anyone preparing for their PPL (Balloons) examination.

AIR NAVIGATION ORDER (ANO)

The Air Navigation Order is the legal document, enacted by parliament, which contains the written law applicable to aviation in the United Kingdom. It is contained in a Statutory Instrument (1989 No. 2004) and comprises numerous 'Articles' relating to specific aspects of aviation law, and 'Schedules' which provide amplification of certain of the Articles where necessary.

The nature of the document requires that it be expressed in legal terminology with the consequence that the content is somewhat protracted and not always easily understood. Therefore, the following are a simplified and condensed version of those Articles which are thought to have particular relevance to this manual.

It is emphasised that for the definitive text of any Article or Schedule the source document must be consulted.

Registration of aircraft
With a few special exceptions, a private pilot must not fly any aircraft in the UK unless the aircraft is registered and displays the appropriate markings of the country of registration.

In the **General Classification of Aircraft** which need to be registered, a balloon (captive or free flying) falls in the category:

Lighter than air aircraft — non-power driven

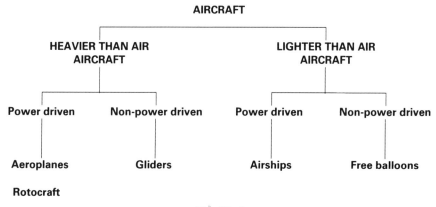

Fig. 28–1

It is the responsibility of the **registered owner** or part-owner to inform the CAA of any changes in the particulars of registration of their aircraft. i.e. change of ownership or withdrawal from use.

Rules of the Air
This is 'Article 64' of the ANO. Individual rules are referred to by number for identification. i.e Rule 5, Rule 7, etc. They are applicable to all aircraft in the UK and to all UK registered aircraft anywhere in the world.

Obviously not all rules can apply to balloons because of their limited speed and directional control, unlike most other aircraft which can choose to fly from one airfield to another along a predictable route, following recognised procedures. However, in the interests of flight safety a balloonist does need to know the rules, to avoid conflict with them and the aircraft abiding by them.

Airworthiness
A **Certificate of Airworthiness** (C of A) is not a compulsory requirement for a balloon flown under the 'private' category. However, in some cases, where a balloon has been issued with a C of A the insurance cover could be in question if the C of A became invalid for any reason. To maintain a current C of A a balloon must be inspected annually by a BBAC appointed

Inspector (or every 100 hours if sooner). A C of A will specify the categories in which the balloon may be operated — Transport, Aerial Work, or Private — and the flight manual which forms part of the C of A must state the necessary requirements, procedures and limitations for the C of A to remain valid during tethering, dropping parachutists, releasing hang-gliders etc.

Pre-flight Actions

Before each flight a pilot-in-command (PIC) must be satisfied that:

The **flight can be made safely** taking into account weather reports and forecasts and that there are options available should it not be possible to complete the flight as planned.

Necessary equipment — altimeter, clock/watch — is functioning correctly and that the appropriate maps and charts are carried.

The aircraft is fit for the flight — any defects since the previous flight have been rectified.

Sufficient fuel is carried for the flight, plus a reserve.

The **aircraft is capable** of performing safely — careful attention being paid to the load chart and the factors affecting lift to ensure the balloon is not overloaded.

All the required **pre-take off checks** have been carried out.

Parachuting

No-one can drop to the surface or jump from an aircraft, other than in an emergency, without the written permission of the CAA. The aircraft must also have provision to do so written into its C of A.

Drunkenness in aircraft

A person must not board an aircraft when drunk, or be drunk in it. (Boarding a balloon when drunk could be a difficult task to accomplish!)

Flying exhibitions

Where such an event requires that the organisers have CAA permission participating PICs must hold a **Display Authorisation** issued by the CAA.

Tethering

A captive balloon must not be flown at more than 60 metres above the ground or within 5 km of an aerodrome except with the written permission of the CAA. Tethering must also be within the scope of the balloon's C of A.

RULES OF THE AIR

These rules apply to all aircraft in the UK and all UK registered aircraft wherever they may be. Deviation from them is only allowed in the case of emergencies or to comply with the law of the land over which the aircraft is flying.

Low flying (Rule 5)

Flight over a congested area. An aircraft (with the exception of helicopters) must fly at such a height over a congested area that would allow it to land clear of the area in the event of engine failure, without danger to people or property; or at 1500 ft or more above the highest fixed object within 2000 ft of the aircraft; whichever is the higher.

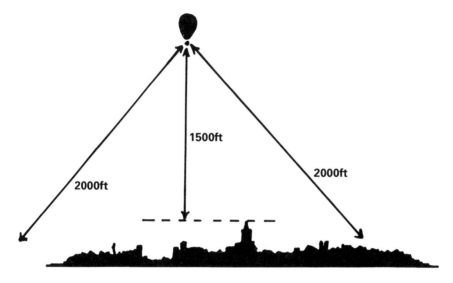

Fig. 28–2   1500 ft rule

Open-Air Gathering. Aircraft shall not fly within 3000 ft of an open-air gathering of more than 1000 people except with CAA permission and the written consent of the organiser.

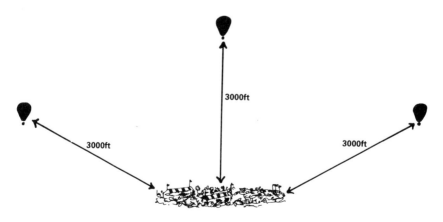

Fig. 28–3   Flight over open air gathering

This rule and the 500 ft rule (below) does not apply when the event is an air race, contest or exhibition of flying authorised by the CAA and the flight made with the organiser's consent.

500 ft rule
An aircraft must not fly closer than 500 ft to any person, vessel, vehicle or structure, except when the aircraft is landing or taking off 'in accordance with normal aviation practice'.

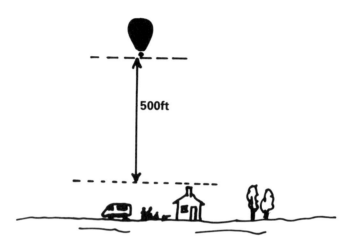

Fig. 28–4   500 ft rule

Aerial Collision Avoidance (Rule 17)
In general terms it is the responsibility of the pilot in command to ensure that he does not collide with another aircraft.

However, since balloons cannot make course or height deviations with any speed, they are bottom of the league when it comes to who should give way when two aircraft are converging. It is debatable whether there would be time to put this rule to the test if a fast jet travelling at several hundred miles per hour suddenly spotted a balloon on its track — if indeed there would be time for the pilot even to spot the balloon in the first place!

An aircraft which is being overtaken has the right of way.

Visual Flight Rules (VFR)
This applies to flight outside controlled airspace and outside special rules airspace.

An aircraft may fly under VFR **above 3000 ft** if it can remain —
> — **1 nm horizontally** and **1000 ft vertically** clear of cloud with a flight visibility of 5 nm

Below 3000 ft an aircraft — other than a helicopter — with a speed of less than 140 kt may fly under VFR if it can remain —
> — **clear of cloud** — **in sight of the surface** with a flight visibility of **1.5 nm** — **without passengers** or a flight visibility of **3 nm** — **with passengers**.

Flight in controlled airspace is generally conducted under **Instrument Flight Rules** (IFR) where the PIC must hold an Instrument Rating. Where traffic and weather conditions allow, ATC can give **Special VFR** (SVFR) clearance for a balloon pilot to enter Control Zones or Special Rules Airspace. With this clearance the balloon must be able to remain **clear of cloud, in sight of surface** with a flight visibility of **5 nm**.

ACCIDENT INVESTIGATION REGULATIONS

An accident must be reported if:–

— anyone in or on the aircraft is killed or seriously injured; unless this is a result of natural causes or inflicted by themselves or other persons

— the aircraft suffers damage which requires major repair

or

— the aircraft is missing or completely inaccessible.

Such accidents must be reported to **The Department of Transport Accident Investigation Branch** by the PIC or, if he is killed or seriously injured, the operator.

If the accident occurs in the UK the local police authority must be informed.

AERONAUTICAL INFORMATION SERVICE (AIS)

One of the functions of the CAA is to provide an Aeronautical Information Service to promote safety and efficiency in aviation. This is done via three main channels:–

— The **U**nited **K**ingdom **A**eronautical **I**nformation **P**ublication **(UK AIP)**

— **NOTAMs** — **NOT**ices to **A**ir**M**en

— **A**eronautical **I**nformation **C**irculars — **AICs**

UK AIP (The Air Pilot) contains information/instruction filling three volumes, under the headings:

AGA — Aerodromes and Ground Aids
COM — Radio Communications and Navigation Facilities
MET — Meteorological Services
RAC — Rules of the Air and Air Traffic Services
FAL — Facilitation (Customs/Immigration etc.)
SAR — Search and Rescue
MAP — relevant Maps and Charts
GEN — general items

NOTAMs are information supplementary to UK AIP — published weekly with details of aeronautical facilities, services, procedures or hazards. Class II NOTAMS are sent through the post while Class I Notams are those of a more urgent nature and are sent via teleprinter.

AICs are issued monthly by the AIS and relate to matters concerned with:–

White — Administration matters; examination dates, new or amendments to publications, course fees etc.
Yellow — Operational matters.
Pink — Safety matters.

Mauve   — amendments to UK airspace restrictions charts.
Green   — Maps and charts.

CIVIL AVIATION PUBLICATIONS
These are published to present information from CAA documents in a more simplified form for the private pilot, including —

       CAP53   — The Student Pilots and Private Pilots Licence
       CAP85   — A guide to Aviation Law
       CAP413   — Radio Telephony Procedures

AIR TRAFFIC RULES AND SERVICES
In the UK airspace is divided into lower airspace and upper airspace.

Lower Airspace — below flight level 245 — comprises of two regions, the London Flight Information Region (FIR) and the Scottish FIR.

Upper Airspace — at and above flight level 245 — has the same geographic regions, the London Upper Flight Information Region (UFR) and the Scottish UFR.

Within these regions are various areas of regulated airspace:–

       Control Zone CTR — an airspace from ground level to a specified altitude or flight level within which ATC service is provided to all flights conducted under IFR, or SVFR in some instances.

       Control Area CTA — an airspace extending from a specified altitude or flight level to an upper flight level limit. Such airspace when established in the vicinity of a major aerodrome is known as a **Terminal Manoeuvring Control Area** (TMA).

An **airway** is a CTA 'corridor'. Identified by a letter and number an airway extends 5nm or more each side of a straight line between two places within specified vertical limits.

i.e. A1 FL65 — FL245 is airway A1 which runs along between 6500ft and 24500ft.

Special Rules Area (SRA) — is airspace in which aircraft must comply with ATC instructions and any other regulations relating to that airspace, from a specified altitude or flight level to an upper limit.

Special Rules Zone (SRZ) — as SRA above but extends from ground level up to a specified altitude or flight level.

Aerodrome Traffic Zone (ATZ) — is airspace at specific types of

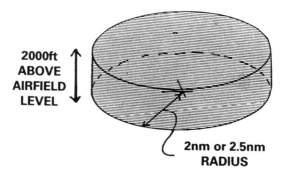

2000ft
ABOVE
AIRFIELD
LEVEL

2nm or 2.5nm
RADIUS

Fig. 28–5 ATZ

aerodrome with an upward extension of **2000 ft** above the airfield and a radius of **2 nm** based on the midpoint of the longest runway if the runway is **1850 m or less** in length. If the runway is **longer than 1850 m** then the radius is **2.5 nm**.

Military Aerodrome Traffic Zone (MATZ) — established at certain military aerodromes where the airspace extends upwards to **3000ft** above the airfield with a radius of **5 nm** centred on the longest runway. There will also be one or more **'stubs'** which are **4 nm wide** extending **5nm along** final approach paths **between 1000 ft–3000 ft** agl. Although technically this is non-regulated airspace a pilot is strongly advised to seek permission to penetrate a MATZ. It must also be borne in mind that there is an ATZ at the centre of this airspace which must be observed.

Two or more MATZ may be amalgamated to produce a **Combined Military Aerodrome Traffic Zone** (CMATZ) with a single controlling authority.

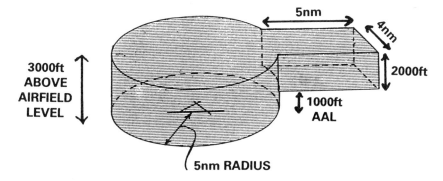

Fig. 28–6   MATZ

SEARCH AND RESCUE SIGNALS
For use to attract attention of search aircraft —

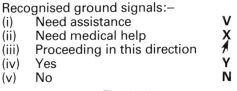

Recognised ground signals:–

(i)	Need assistance	**V**
(ii)	Need medical help	**X**
(iii)	Proceeding in this direction	**↗**
(iv)	Yes	**Y**
(v)	No	**N**

Fig. 28–7

29

NAVIGATION

Navigation is defined as the skill of steering a ship or aircraft on its set course. In ballooning the meaning really boils down to the skill of identifying the course the aircraft is taking. We need to know where we are at any precise moment, and where we have been. Using this information we can then predict where we might be going!

To pinpoint a location anywhere in the world, the globe is divided by imaginary lines.

Those which run north to south are semicircles identified as degrees east or degrees west of the 0° line which passes through Greenwich, up to 180° which is on the opposite side of the globe. These lines are known as meridians of **longitude**.

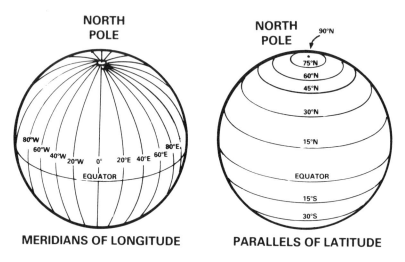

Fig. 29–1   Meridians of longitude — parallels of latitude

The lines which run east and west are circles around the globe known as parallels of **latitude**. These are measured in degrees, north or south of the equator.

Each degree can be subdivided into sixty minutes. The distance between minutes of latitude is one nautical mile.

The UK itself has been divided up into one kilometre squares known as the **National Grid** which simplifies map references.

Maps & Charts

There are three basic types of map or chart used by balloonists.

Topographical charts: I.C.A.O. UK Aeronautical charts, 1:500,000
Topographical charts: I.C.A.O. UK Aeronautical charts, 1:250,000
Ordnance Survey maps: Landranger series, 1:50,000

The scale of a map is shown as a ratio of what one unit on the map represents on the ground.

1:500,000   1 cm on map = 500,000 cm on the ground (5 km)
                 1 in on map = 500,000 in on the ground (approx 8 miles)

1:250,000   1 cm on map = 250,000 cm on ground (2.5 km)
                 1 in on map = 250,000 in on the ground (approx 4 miles)

1:50,000   1 cm on map = 50,000 cm on ground (.5 km)
                 1 in on map = 50,000 in on the ground (.8 mile)

All these charts carry a scale showing distances in statute miles, kilometres and nautical miles.

U.K. Aeronautical Chart — 1:500,000

Because of the scale this is often referred to as the half million chart.

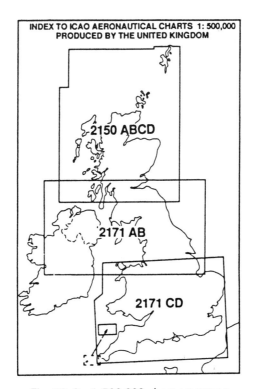

Fig. 29–2   1:500,000 chart coverage

Latitude and longitude are used for reference. Overlaid on this chart is all the surface air information as well as the above surface air information for the area covered. The UK is covered by three charts:
— Scotland, Orkney and Shetland
— Northern England
— Southern England.
These charts are updated every one to two years.

The airspace information needs to be interpreted three dimensionally which sounds complicated but is relatively straightforward in practice. All aviators need to know how to use this chart to comply with the rules of the air and to avoid infringement of controlled airspace. There is no short cut to understanding the information other than learning all the signs and symbols used, and their meanings. However they are not too numerous and should be easily memorised.

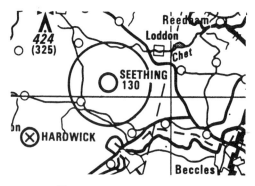

Fig. 29–3   ATZ on chart

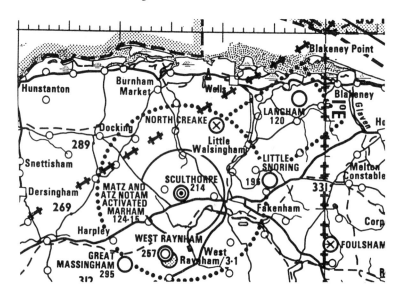

Fig. 29–4   MATZ on chart

An Aerodrome Traffic Zone (ATZ) appears as a circle on the map but the regulated airspace at this point extends from the surface up to 2000 ft above the aerodrome (AAL) for a radius of 2 nm from the centre of the main runway if its length is 1850 m or less, or 2.5 nm if the runway is longer.

A Military Aerodrome Traffic Zone (MATZ) also appears as a circle but with one or more stubs projecting. The area within the circle, extends from the surface up to 3000 ft AAL and has a larger radius of 5 nm. A stub however, which is 5 nm long and 4 nm wide, does not extend from the surface but from 1000ft up to 3000 ft.

In general, information on the map referred to as a 'zone' extends from the surface upwards to a given height or altitude and an 'area' starts at a height above the surface and extends to an upper limit.

UK AERONAUTICAL CHART — 1:250,000
Referred to as the quarter million chart. Latitude and longitude are used for reference between this chart and the half million, but the National Grid is also shown which is useful for reference to O.S. maps. This series covers the UK in eighteen overlapping sheets. With a scale of roughly four miles to the inch this chart is more practical for ballooning. However, it only shows aeronautical information at or below 3000 ft. For flight above this level the half million chart must be referred to.

These charts are normally revised every two to three years.

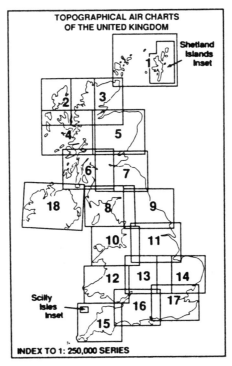

Fig. 29–5   1:250,000 chart coverage

ORDNANCE SURVEY LANDRANGER SERIES — 1:50,000

The O.S. map. — covers Britain using 204 sheets. This is the map preferred by balloonists for in-flight navigation. All land features are clearly marked, roads, villages, woods, and power lines etc. (even pubs and phone boxes!) so there is little excuse for getting lost. The National Grid is marked on these charts which means a map reference can be given to locate a point to within about 100 metres.

Obviously a pilot needs to be able to translate information from the air-charts to the O.S. chart in use. To save time and also to avoid having to use more than one map at once in the confines of the basket, the information can be drawn directly on to the O.S. chart. A Ballooning Calculator can facilitate this task, and the use of fluorescent highlight pens makes the information easy to spot without obliterating other information on the map. Bear in mind that the 1:250,000 charts only carry air information up to 3000 ft and for information above that the appropriate 1:500,000 chart should be consulted.

BBAC/Landowner sensitive areas should also be marked on maps. These areas are published in booklet form and regularly updated by means of the BBAC *Pilots Circular*.

Charts overprinted with air and/or sensitive areas information are now available through the BBAC — Map Printing Services. (See Appendix 3.)

Map reading

It is a requirement for the flight test that a pilot is able to navigate, and knowledge of the balloon's whereabouts is the pilot's responsibility. However, a pilot may delegate the map reading to another person in the basket if he so wishes on subsequent flights.

A crew member proficient at map reading and familiar with the charts used could find their own flight training easier to cope with having had this experience.

An essential skill when using these charts is the ability to read map or grid references. A pilot must be able to locate points in relation to the information he is marking on a map such as the BBAC/NFU sensitive areas and air information. It is also necessary for both pilot and retrieve crew to understand a grid reference to locate the landing site of a 'lost' balloon, or to understand where the vehicle must enter an area in order to locate the balloon.

For some people the mention of a map reference creates a panic but it is quite a straightforward and logical exercise.

The National Grid

The whole of the UK has been divided up into 100 kilometre (100,000 metre) squares which are identified by two letters. These squares are then subdivided into kilometre squares identified by numbers. Since a standard chart only covers 40 x 40 kilometres square and often overlaps its neigh-bours, balloonists usually omit reference to these two letter references and use instead the number of the sheet in use.

The six figure reference for the junction on the map below is arrived at as follows:–

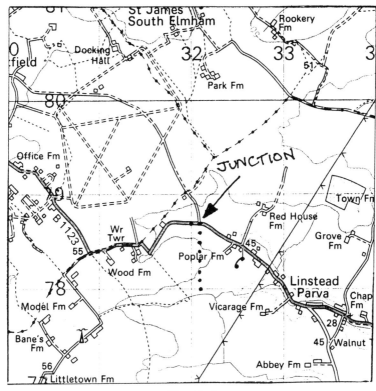

Fig. 29–6

Sheet 156

The first three figures are 'Eastings' —
Read the grid line to the lEft — or the vertical line
This will give you two figures.
Estimate how many 'tenths' into the square the point is to
arrive at the third figure.

321

The second three figures are 'Northings' —
Read the grid line below — or the horizontal line
Estimate how many 'tenths' the point is above this line to
arrive at the third figure.

787

The reference would therefore be given as: *Sheet 156 ref: 321787*

A Ballooning Calculator has on one corner a 'roamer' which when laid on the point in question will give you the tenths or the third figure in each direction, eliminating the guesswork.

Direction
The direction of travel is expressed in degrees, which starts at North — 0°,
and passes full circle clockwise through 360°. (East = 090°, South = 180°,
West = 270°.)

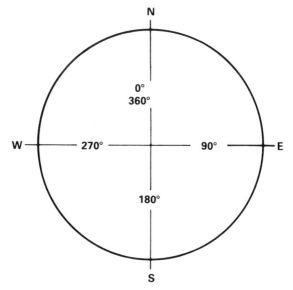

Fig. 29–7   Compass points

   Unfortunately a compass does not point to the true north but several
degrees to one side. The compass points to magnetic north and this varies
with time and place. In 1990 magnetic deviation was 6° to the west of true
north in this country and it is decreasing by 9 minutes annually. (1° = 60
minutes) Directions should therefore be given with the suffix 'T' for true or
'M' for magnetic, and the necessary allowances made.

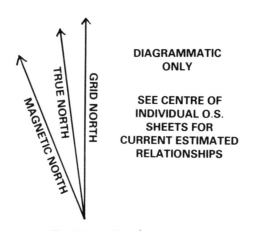

Fig. 29–8   North deviations

30

METEOROLOGY

A good understanding of meteorology is an essential part of every balloon pilot's education. To recognise safe and suitable conditions for ballooning a pilot must be able to interpret the current situation correctly from weather charts and preceding weather patterns. To do this a little groundwork on the basics of weather is necessary.

Atmosphere
The earth is enveloped by a mixture of gases known as the atmosphere. These gases consist of two layers, the lower **troposphere** and the upper **stratosphere**. The division of the two layers, which occurs at 60,000 feet above the equator and 20,000 feet over the two poles, is known as the **tropopause**. However an average height of 36,000 ft is generally taken as this division. Most 'weather' occurs in the troposphere while conditions in the stratosphere are far more consistent and stable.

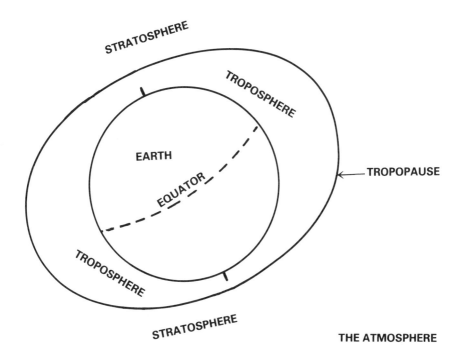

Fig. 30–1   The atmosphere

The atmosphere is composed of a mixture of gases, mainly:
oxygen 21%
nitrogen 78%
other gases 1%
plus water vapour — in varying quantities
'Weather' is the result of three main influences on the atmosphere —
heat, moisture, and pressure.

Heat

The sun supplies energy to the earth in the form of radiant heat. Uneven
absorption of this heat gives rise to currents in the atmosphere, which in
turn results in the changing weather patterns experienced around the
globe.

Heat waves from the sun radiate through the atmosphere to be
absorbed by the earth's surface. Some surfaces absorb heat readily —
such as sand and rocks, while others are slow to heat up — like woodlands
and water, or reflect the heat — like snow. Other factors can also affect the
rise in temperature of the surface i.e. the latitude of the location, the
season, and time of day.

Cloud can have an effect on heat reaching the surface. In daytime cloud
cover can absorb some of the sun's radiation and prevent it reaching the
earth's surface. At night, when there is no heat from the sun, heat
absorbed during the day is radiated upwards and the surface cools. In
winter clear skies at night can lead to very cold frosty mornings but in
cloudy conditions this heat is trapped by the cloud layer, arresting the
cooling effect.

Air in contact with a warm surface will absorb heat. This air will rise and
colder air will be drawn in setting up convection currents in the
atmosphere.

The sea breeze effect demonstrates this on a small scale. By day, land
absorbs heat more readily than sea. The air above the land warms up and
rises. This draws in air from the cooler area. Air above the water sinks to
replace this and draws air from the warmer area. The cool air warms and
the warm air cools in this circulation pattern keeping the rotation going,
and an onshore surface breeze develops.

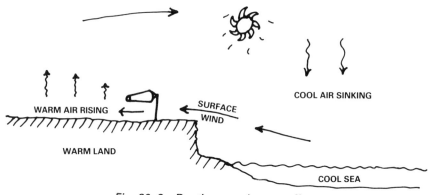

Fig. 30–2 Daytime sea breeze effect

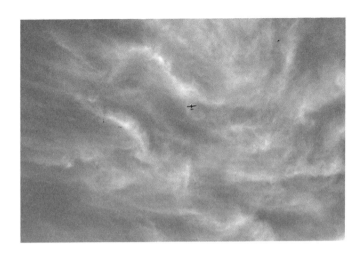

*Filaments of
Cirrus (Ci).*

Cirrostratus (Cs).

*Altostratus (As),
thickening towards
horizon; Cu fractus
below.*

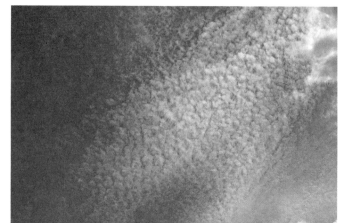

Altocumulus (Ac).

Nimbostratus (Ns).

Stratocumulus (Sc).

*Stratus (St);
terrain (and TV
mast!) in cloud.*

Cumulus (Cu).

*Large Cumulus
build-up;
(showers and poor
visibility below).*

*Mature
Cumulonimbus (Cb);
(avoid Cb clouds,
with or without
anvil).*

*Ac Castellanus
formation.*

*Lenticular
Altocumulus.*

At night the reverse happens. The land cools more rapidly, so the sea is the warmer area causing the surface breeze to flow from the land out to sea.

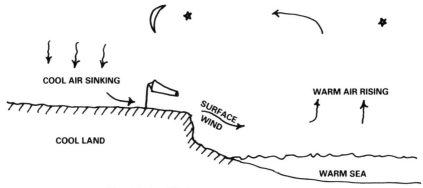

Fig. 30–3   Night-time sea breeze effect

Similar heating patterns affect hills and valleys. At night, cooling air sinks as the tops of the hills cool quicker than the land in the base of valleys creating what is known as **katabatic wind**.

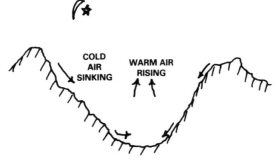

Fig. 30–4   Katabatic wind

In the sunshine the warm air rises up the sides of the hillside. This is known as an **anabatic wind**.

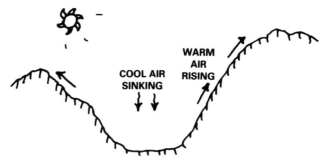

Fig. 30–5   Anabatic wind

Temperature

Because the atmosphere is heated from below by radiation from the earth's surfaces, temperature normally decreases with height at approximately 2°C for every 1000 ft up to 36,000 ft (the tropopause) where it levels out to a constant −55°C. This is known as the **lapse rate**.

When compression of air occurs its temperature will rise (the heat generated when using a bicycle pump demonstrates this) and conversely, when air expands its temperature drops. These are known as adiabatic temperature changes.

Dry adiabatic lapse rate: the rate of cooling as dry air rises
= 3°C per 1000 ft.
Wet adiabatic lapse rate: the rate of cooling of rising moist air (this is reduced because latent heat is released as water vapour condenses)
= 1°C per 1000 ft

Moisture

Air can absorb water, in vapour form, in increasing quantities until a saturation point is reached. Warm air has a greater capacity for holding moisture than cooler air. Therefore a mass of warm air, not at saturation point, on cooling down will eventually reach a temperature where it is saturated and if it cools further some of the water vapour will not be contained and will **condense** into visible water droplets forming a cloud. The point of saturation is known as the '**dew point**'. The quantity of moisture in a given mass of air is known as the relative **humidity**, therefore 100% humidity = saturation = dew point.

Air travelling over continental land masses will be relatively dry even if cool because there is little moisture to absorb but over oceans air will contain high quantities of moisture.

Pressure

Imagine a column of air. The lower molecules are compressed by the weight of those above. Working upwards, the weight bearing down from above decreases and the molecules are less densely packed together. It can be seen therefore, that the pressure decreases with height and so does the density of the air.

This decrease in density means that the air will become 'thinner' with height and therefore will contain less oxygen by volume. For flights above 10,000 ft there will not be sufficient oxygen to support normal breathing and an additional oxygen supply will be needed. The efficiency of the balloon burner will also be affected, since combustion is dependent on oxygen.

Pressure is still measured in the UK in **millibars** (mb) although the same unit is now known worldwide as a **hectopascal** (hPa). On a 'standard day' the pressure at sea level is 1013.2 mb. At low levels, decrease in pressure with altitude can be taken as 1 mb per 30 ft. Pressure readings taken at different locations are all reduced to the equivalent pressure reading at sea level. Weather maps are then drawn up showing lines linking areas of similar sea-level pressure. These lines are **isobars** and appear rather like contour lines on a map, indicating areas of high or low pressure as opposed to high or low lying land features.

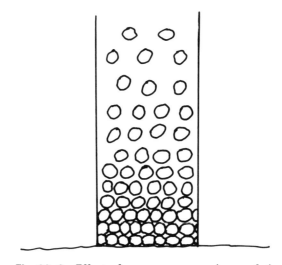

Fig. 30–6   Effect of pressure on a column of air

On a weather chart, isobars are usually drawn at 2-8 mb intervals. If they are close together the pressure gradient is said to be steep or strong and if widely spaced the gradient is flat or weak. An area of high pressure is known as a high or **anticyclone** and a low pressure area is a low or **depression**. The map can also show a **trough** of low pressure or a **ridge** of high pressure. An area of fairly even pressure between a pair of lows and a pair of highs is referred to as a col.

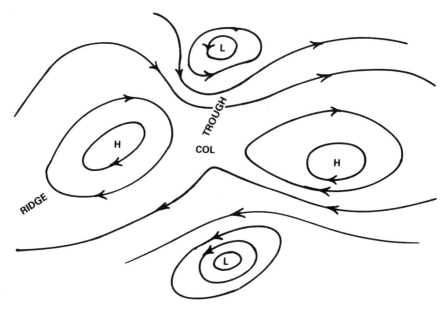

Fig. 30–7   Isobars

Depressions are typically areas of bad weather with wind speed increasing towards the centre, while anticyclones are areas of better weather — more settled with winds decreasing towards the centre.

Altimeter settings

Since an altimeter works on the same principal as a barometer, giving a reading relative to the actual pressure experienced by the instrument, an aircraft could experience different readings flying through areas of varying pressures although the aircraft maintained a constant height. An altimeter can be set to a given pressure so that all aircraft in the same area will be flying on the same height scale. The UK is divided into regions which take the lowest forecast pressure as the **regional QNH**. When flying from one region to another the altimeter has to be reset to the new QNH setting. The relatively short length of a balloon flight seldom requires this procedure.

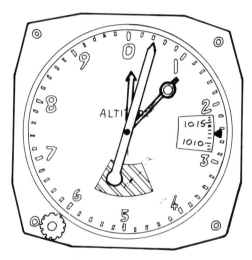

Fig. 30–8   Altimeter

An altimeter set on a **QNH** pressure shows a vertical distance in feet above mean sea level — this is known as **altitude**.

If an altimeter is set to an airfield's **QFE** this gives a reading as the **height above the airfield**.

Above the **transition altitude** — 3000 ft — a single standard altimeter setting of 1013 mb is used and the altimeter reading is referred to as a **Flight Level** (FL). A flight level is expressed in hundreds of feet and so 8000 ft is known as FL80, 4500 ft as FL45 etc. This pressure setting is referred to as **QNE**.

Temperatures and pressures are constantly changing and an average set of values for sea level have been taken, known as the **International Standard Atmosphere** (ISA):

$$pressure = 1013.2 \text{ mb (hPa)}$$
$$temperature = +15°C$$
$$air density = 1225 \text{ gm/cubic metre}$$

Wind speed

This is generally given as knots (nautical miles per hour) in aviation forecasts but other forecasts often use the Beaufort wind scale, a classification pioneered by Admiral Beaufort. General forecasts often use a much wider classification such as 'light', 'moderate', or 'strong'.

Windspeeds/Scales

Description	speed in knots	Beaufort scale	General forecast
Calm	less than 1	0	calm
Light air	1–3	1	⎫
Light breeze	4–6	2	⎬ light
Gentle breeze	7–10	3	⎭
Moderate breeze	11–16	4	moderate
Fresh breeze	17–21	5	fresh
Strong breeze	22–27	6	⎫ strong
Moderate gale	28–33	7	
Fresh gale	34–40	8	gale
Strong gale	41–47	9	⎫
Whole gale	48–55	10	⎬ severe gale or storm
Storm	56–63	11	
Hurricane	64–71	12	⎭

Local variations

In some areas it will be found that the winds do not comply with the direction of isobars or Buys Ballot's Law. This can be due to disturbances produced by land features, such as hills and valleys giving rise to anabatic or katabatic winds; or the effect of land and sea breezes.

Air flowing over the top of a hill becomes compressed and the result is an increase of speed in the flow at this point. Something to be aware of if contemplating a landing in such an area.

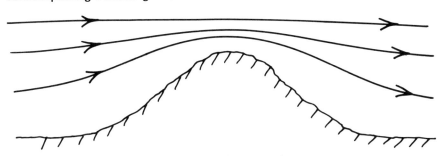

Fig. 30–13 Compression

Buys Ballot's Law

This states 'If you stand with your back to the wind in the Northern Hemisphere, the Low pressure will be on your Left.'

Another useful point for balloonists to remember is that changes in wind direction tend to be 'right with height' and 'low to the left'.

Fig. 30–11

Wind direction

Wind direction is the direction from which the wind is blowing. It can be given in degrees, or as a compass point. i.e. a wind blowing from south to north is given as 180° (true) or a southerly direction.

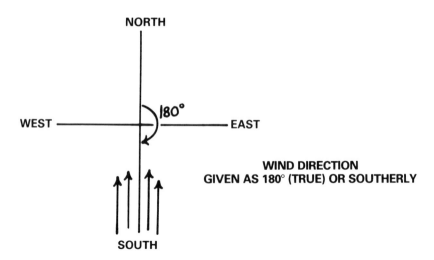

Fig. 30–12 Wind direction

Wind

Generally this term means the horizontal flow of air over the surface. Wind is the flow of air from a column of high pressure to one of low pressure. The winds resulting from a strong gradient (isobars close together) will be stronger than from a weaker one. However the wind does not flow perpendicular to the isobars from high to low pressure as one would expect. If it did the different pressure areas would level out and there would be no more flow at all. The rotation of the earth also has an influence on the flow — the **coriolis force** and tries to turn wind to the right in the northern hemisphere. The faster the winds, the greater this effect. Eventually the two effects balance one another and the wind follows the line of the isobars — the **geostrophic effect**.

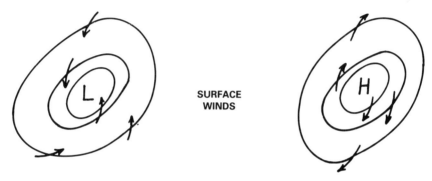

Fig. 30–9   Surface winds

Friction with the surface has a slowing effect so the ground wind speeds will generally be less than the upper ones. Also, at ground level, wind flows at 5° to 15° to the isobars:

— towards a low
— outwards from a high.

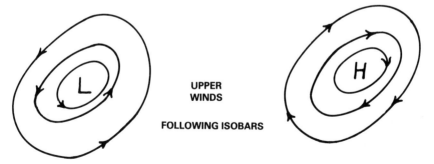

Fig. 30–10   Upper winds

At 1500 ft or so the winds blow along the isobars. Around a low pressure system the wind flow is anti-clockwise and around high pressure the flow is clockwise.

Funnelling can happen when wind enters a valley. This will take the wind in the direction of the feature and again there will possibly be an increase in speed due to the effects of compression.

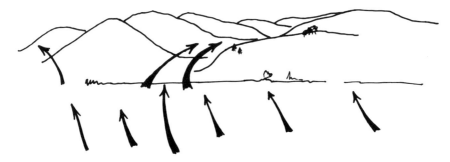

Fig. 30–14   Funnelling

Some features will create **turbulence** in air flowing over and around them. Turbulence increases with windspeed — an important factor to bear in mind if flying in windspeeds greater than about 15 knots. Down-draughts caused by curl-over in the 'wind shadow' of hillsides or wooded areas can also become quite vigorous in fast conditions, sometimes forcing a balloon into an unpremeditated descent with no time to round out and avoid a hard ground contact.

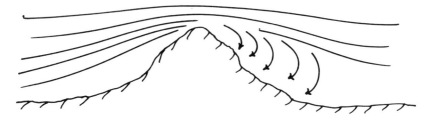

Fig. 30–15   Curl-over

Windshear
This is an unexpected variation in windspeed and/or direction, sometimes encountered during a balloon flight. The balloon may experience an unexpected change of direction and or a speeding up or slowing down of the rate of travel. In extreme cases the turbulence will be quite severe and an envelope could be partially flattened before it can be stabilised in the new conditions. Heat needs to be applied without delay to counteract the loss of air from the envelope.

Cloud
Clouds consist of tiny droplets of water and/or ice crystals, formed when rising moist air cools below dew point and its water vapour condenses. They can be a visible indication of what is actually happening in the atmosphere and a pointer to what can be expected to follow.

Air can rise in the following ways:
> by convection — from surface heating
> orographically — over hills and mountains
> as mass lift — within depressions and along fronts
> as a result of windshear — from the turbulence it causes

There are four main groups of cloud:
> cirroform — thin and wispy
> cumuliform — lumpy heaps
> stratiform — layers
> nimbus — rain cloud

Different types occur at three general levels:

High level clouds: formed from ice crystals with bases above 20,000 ft.

Cirrus (Ci) — featherlike wisps or mares' tails, produced by mass lift, and occasionally by turbulence, this cloud is often to be seen as the approach of a front. Can indicate that winds will increase in a few hours.

Cirrostratus (Cs) — veil-like milky layer. Again formed by mass lift, it is the only cloud to produce haloes around the sun or moon. Can also be an indication of the approach of a front.

Cirrocumulus (Cc) — a spread of small white 'lumps' often referred to as a mackerel sky. Not significant of any weather change. Cloud formed by turbulence.

Medium level clouds: composed of a mixture of water vapour and ice crystals, with bases above 6500 ft

Altostratus (As) — a dull grey covering almost obscuring the sun. Caused by mass lift, usually associated with a front.

Altocumulus (Ac) — similar to cirrocumulus but 'lumps' are larger and greyish-white. Again often known as a mackerel sky. No particular weather associations, but frequently caused by turbulence.

Low level clouds: formed from water vapour with bases below 6500 ft

Nimbostratus (Ns) — as its name suggests, a layer of rain bearing cloud. It obscures the sun and appears grey, often lacking a distinct lower surface due to falling rain (or snow). Produced by mass lift.

Stratus (St) — a thin grey layer produced by turbulence or orographically.

Cumulus (Cu) — detached lumpy clouds formed vertically, generally by convection. Typical tops look like cauliflowers, brilliant white in the sunlight, while bases are darker because sun cannot penetrate through. A clear indication of an unstable atmosphere with the larger cumulus sometimes producing showers. The surface winds become gusty and directions variable.

Cumulonimbus (Cb) — a really huge cumulus cloud. The base of the cloud will appear dark and stormy while the top, which can extend up as far as the tropopause, or even higher in the tropics, takes on the characteristic 'anvil' shape. A result of very strong convection, this is the cloud which produces thunderstorms and hail. The strong up and down currents in this type of cloud are very hazardous to all forms of aviation. It should also be appreciated that the storm cloud is only the visible portion of the turbulence and the associated strong up-draughts and down-draughts can extend beyond this.

In addition to these general cloud formations **lenticular clouds** (lens shaped) are of interest to balloonists. These form in **lee waves** which are a type of turbulence created by wind flowing across a range of mountains or hills. A wave motion is set up on the downwind side. Moist air moving up to the crest of a wave may cool enough to form cloud and as it sinks to a trough it warms and the cloud evaporates. Therefore although the air is travelling along the wave pattern, the cloud appears to be stationary. The ground level wind beneath this type of cloud formation will be very turbulent, often indicated by small 'rotor' clouds at lower level. The wave effect can travel a considerable distance downwind.

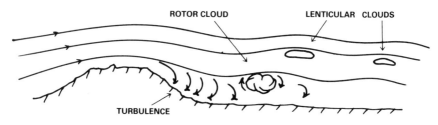

Fig. 30–16   Lenticular cloud

Precipitation
This is a general term for the water from clouds, arriving at the surface in the form of rain, hail, snow, sleet or drizzle. The type of precipitation can help with cloud identification.

    Showers generally fall from cumulus cloud.
    Continuous rain from stratus types.
    Very heavy rain, hailstones from cumulonimbus.

Thermals
The formation of small white fluffy cumulus clouds as a result of convection during warm weather indicates the presence of thermal activity and therefore unstable conditions for ballooning.

    A **thermal** starts as a 'bubble' of air formed on the surface of an area which is warmer than its surroundings. It gradually builds up until it pops up free from the surface. Being warm it rises, and as a result cold air flows in below.

    The upward travel of a thermal can be deflected by windshear and as a result a balloon can experience dramatic changes in lateral as well as vertical direction. Turbulent effects can severely distort an envelope causing it to lose volume and heat. At height there is time to reheat the envelope and round out from any resulting descent, but similar conditions at low level can make approaches and landings very hazardous.

Visibility
This refers to the clarity of the air. In really clear conditions visibility can be as far as 100 nm.

    Various factors can reduce visibility:
        Dust particles in the air can cause haze, as seen when combine harvesters are busy in the fields during harvest.

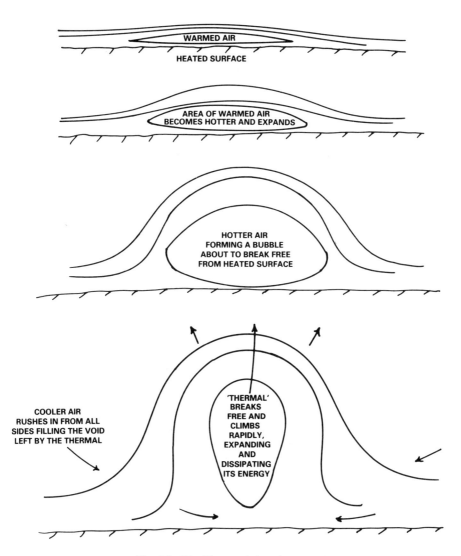

Fig. 30–17 Thermal development

Visibility

This refers to the clarity of the air. In really clear conditions visibility can be as far as 100 nm.

Various factors can reduce visibility:

Dust particles in the air can cause haze, as seen when combine harvesters are busy in the fields during harvest.

Water droplets as moist air cools below dew point at low level, producing mist (visibility of over 1000 m) or fog (visibility less than 1000 m).

Sand lifted by strong winds.

Precipitation — rain, drizzle, hail or snow; the heavier the downfall the more reduced the visibility.

Smoke in heavy industrial areas can become trapped in the lower air producing haze, as can smoke from burning stubble at harvest time. Smoke trapped in foggy conditions is known as smog.

Inversion

This occurs when a layer of cold air is capped by a layer of warm air which acts as a lid, preventing moisture which has condensed as a mist in the cold air from dispersing. This results in an increase in temperature with height instead of the usual decrease. A low level temperature could be 5°–8°C less than the temperature at 1000 ft.

Mist and fog

In cooled air moisture condenses into visible water droplets when the saturation point reaches 100% (dew point). In the upper air this appears as cloud but at ground level it is known as mist or fog, depending upon its density. Dew will appear on cold surfaces, fog above.

Mist = Visibility greater than 1000 m
Fog = Visibility less than 1000 m

Radiation Fog occurs when moist air is cooled by the surface losing its heat through radiation, especially in low areas where air may be damper. A light wind is also needed to mix the cooling air in order to bring about the condensation.

Advection fog is the product of windier conditions where moist warm air passes over cold surfaces. Sea fog is an example of this. It forms when the sea is relatively cold in the warmer air conditions of spring or early summer. Sea breezes can carry it inland during the day.

Hill fog arrives 1–2 hours after sunrise as a result of rising radiation fog with an increase in windspeed.

Frontal fog is a result of precipitation or low surface cloud associated with a warm front or occlusion.

Steam fog can sometimes occur on still evenings where cold air flowing over warm damp areas picks up moisture which condenses in the cold layer above.

Frontal weather

Air masses arriving over the UK have differing characteristics influenced by the areas they have passed over en route (Fig. 30–19).

The meeting of two air masses at different temperatures is known as a **front**.

If cold air is being pushed along by warmer air the temperature rises as it passes and it is known as a **warm front**.

If cold air is advancing over warm air and the temperature is dropping it is a **cold front**.

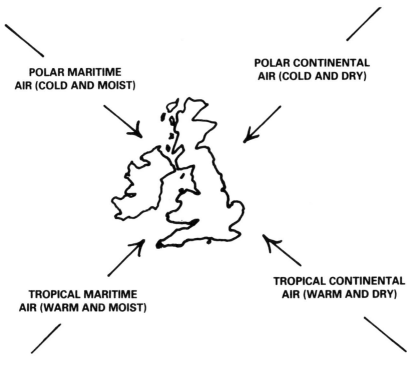

Fig. 30–18   UK influences

Warm front

With a warm front the warmer air climbs over the retreating cold air forming a slope across the division of the two air masses.

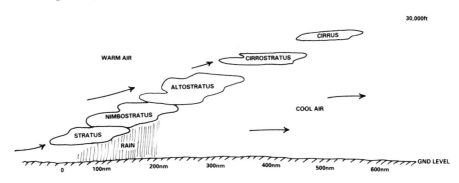

Fig. 30–19   Warm front

Moisture in the warm air condenses as it rises forming cloud. The overlap can be several hundreds of miles wide and at something like 600 miles ahead of the surface front the slope will reach up into the upper troposphere and cirrus clouds will be seen. The cloud thickens as the slope comes nearer the surface. The cirrus will be seen to be followed by cirrostratus, altostratus down to nimbostratus with rain. The belt of rain can be 200–300 miles wide and will be heaviest as the front passes at ground level. Visibility will be poor and there will be the likelihood of fog.

Cold front
With a cold front the advancing cold air pushes in below the warm air forming a steeper slope than a warm front and the resulting band of weather will be much narrower (30–50 miles).

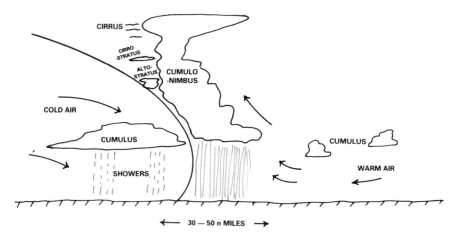

Fig. 30–20   Cold front

As with a warm front the rising warm air will produce similar effects, but here the changes are more rapid because of the steeper slope. Cumulus and cumulonimbus form at the surface front giving heavy rain and storms. Altostratus, cirrostratus and cirrus will occur in a narrow belt behind the front and the sky will often clear quickly.

Other characteristics of a cold front are: falling pressure before, which rises as the front passes, wind that veers and a temperature that rises after the front has passed.

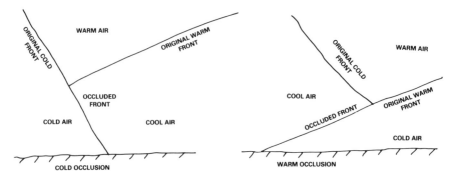

Fig. 30–21   Cold occlusion/warm occlusion

Occluded front

A warm front moves slower than the cold front travelling behind. When the two fronts meet they form what is called an occluded front.

The warm sector is lifted and the front then behaves like a warm or a cold front depending on which is the warmer of the two cold sectors meeting at the surface.

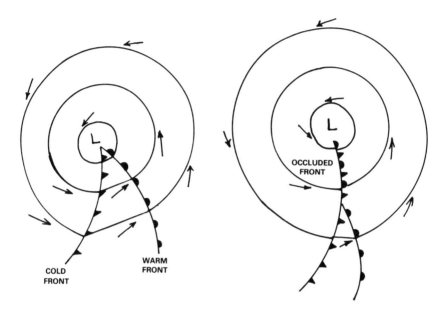

Fig. 30–22   Fronts on weather chart

Forecasts and reports

A **forecast** is an analysis of information received from the numerous weather stations, satellites etc. used to predict what is likely to happen over the next hours, days or weeks. A **report** gives actual weather information at a specific time.

Forecasts

Forecasts appearing in the press, or on radio or television are of limited use for ballooning because of their very general nature. However some press and television forecasts show synoptic charts which can be studied to follow the progress of highs, lows, fronts etc.

AIRMET, a pre-recorded low level forecast is available by telephone, giving a more detailed forecast specifically for aviation. There are three AIRMET regions, Scottish, Northern and Southern (England). The forecast is given at dictation speed, in a standard form which can be transcribed on to an AIRMET copy form. (These are available free of charge, on receipt of SAE — A4 size, from AOPA or Airtour International.) While the information given is geared to aviation in general, a balloonist will need to know more specific surface and lower winds information.

A special forecast for ballooning, supplementary to AIRMET, can be obtained by phone which carries additional information on low level wind speeds/direction etc. This has to be booked in advance from the Bracknell Met Office, or the Manchester or Glasgow Weather Centres.

Reports
A simple weather report sometimes useful in pre-flight planning is **VOLMET**. This is frequently updated information, from selected airfields around the UK broadcast on VHF airband radio. Information given includes surface wind speed and direction, temperature and dew point, cloud cover and QNH.

A handy calculation to give an estimated cloudbase can be done from a VOLMET report. This is effective for morning and early afternoon.

(Air temperature — dew point) x 400 = cloudbase in feet above surface.

APPENDIX 1

ABBREVIATIONS USED

AAL	Above Aerodrome Level
agl	above ground level
amsl	above mean sea level
ANO	Air Navigation Order
ATC	Air Traffic Control
BBAC	British Balloon & Airship Club
CAA	Civil Aviation Authority
cm	centimetre
C of A	Certificate of Airworthiness
CPL	Commercial Pilots Licence
CPL(B)	Commercial Pilots Licence (Balloons)
CTA	Control Area
CTZ	Control Zone
°C	degrees Celcius
FAI	Federation Aeronautique Internationale
FIR	Flight Information Region
FL	flight level
fpm	feet per minute
ft	foot (feet)
ICAO	International Civil Aviation Organisation
IFR	Instrument Flight Rules
IMC	Instrument Meteorological Conditions
in	inch(es)
ISA	International Standard Atmosphere
Kg	kilogramme(s)
Km	kilometre(s)
kt	knot(s)
LRO	Landowners Relations Officer
met.	meteorological
mb	millibars
mm	millimetres
°M	degrees magnetic
NFU	National Farmers Union
nm	nautical miles
O.S.	Ordnance Survey
P/UT	pilot under training
PCZ	prohibited competition zone
PIC	pilot in command
PPL	private pilots licence
PPL(B)	private pilots licence (balloons and airships)
p.u.	polyurethane
PZ	prohibited zone
R/T	radio telephony
SA	sensitive area
SVFR	Special Visual Flight Rules
TMA	Terminal Control Area
UK	United Kingdom
VFR	Visual Flight Rules
VMC	visual met. conditions

APPENDIX 2

ACKNOWLEDGEMENTS

We are grateful for all the help, advice and encouragement we received from our many ballooning friends, and especially from; Ray Bailey, Derek Belton, Pete Bish, Roger Brown, Phil Dunnington, Chris Jolliffe, Kevin Meehan, Ally Odell, Robert Pooley, Bill Ryall, Laurie Ryan, Nigel Tasker, Colin Wolstenholme, BBAC.

The BBAC Pilot Code of Conduct and the BBAC Safety Code, reproduced by kind permission of the BBAC.

Maps and charts , reproduced by kind permission of the Civil Aviation Authority, Ordnance Survey, AOPA.

Photographs supplied by; Airtour International, Airtour Balloon Co., Airlife, Cameron Balloons, Bob Bennett, Gordon Coles, Bob Howes, Thunder & Colt Ltd., Arthur Williams.

APPENDIX 3

USEFUL ADDRESSES

AERONAUTICAL INFORMATION SERVICE
NATS. AIS Central Office, First Floor, Control Tower Building,
Heathrow Airport, Hounslow, Middlesex
Tel: 0272 292480

AERONAUTICAL SECTION, RADIOCOMMUNICATIONS AGENCY
Room 712, Waterloo Bridge House, Waterloo Road, LONDON SE1 8UA
Tel: 081 745 3456

A.O.P.A. UK
50 Cambridge Street, LONDON SW1
Tel: 071 834 5631

BALLOONING EQUIPMENT

AIRTOUR BALLOON COMPANY
Mill Road, Cranfield, BEDFORD, MK43 0JG
Tel: 0234 750890

CAMERON BALLOONS LTD
St Johns Street, Bedminster, BRISTOL BS3 4NH
Tel: 0272 637216

THUNDER & COLT LTD
Maesbury Road, Oswestry, Shropshire SY10 8HA
Tel: 0691 670644

ZEBEDEE BALLOON SERVICE (New & Secondhand)
Pete Bish,
Honeypot Cottage, Beehive Lane, Binfield, Berks. RG12 4TX
Tel: 0344 421527

BALLOON MANUFACTURERS – UK

AIRTOUR BALLOON COMPANY
Mill Road, Cranfield, BEDFORD, MK43 0JG
Tel: 0234 750890

CAMERON BALLOONS LTD
St Johns Street, Bedminster, BRISTOL BS3 4NH
Tel: 0272 637216

THUNDER & COLT LTD
Maesbury Road, Oswestry, Shropshire SY10 8HA
Tel: 0691 670644

BOOKS, MAPS & CHARTS

AEROSHOPPING
50A Cambridge Street, LONDON SW1V 4QQ
Tel: 071 834 9307

AIRTOUR BALLOONS
Mill Road, Cranfield, BEDFORD, MK43 0JG
Tel: 0234 750890

AIRTOUR INTERNATIONAL
Elstree Aerodrome, Herts. WD6 3AW
Tel: 081 953 4870/6064

BBAC SALES
Sue Jones, 39 Kentmere Terrace, Erdington, BIRMINGHAM B5 5RT
Tel: 021 643 3224 (day) 021 377 6245 (evening)

BRITISH BALLOON AND AIRSHIP CLUB

INFORMATION
PO Box 1006
Birmingham B5 5RT
Tel: 021 643 3224

MAP PRINTING SERVICES
Derek Belton
Alder House, Whiteleaf, BUCKS HP17 0LQ
Tel: 0844 274475

MEMBERSHIP
Ann & Roger Brown
1 Shirley Road, Maidenhead, Berks SL6 4PH
Tel: 0628 27204

PILOTS CIRCULAR
Pete Bish,
Honeypot Cottage, Beehive Lane, Binfield, Berks. RG12 4TX
Tel: 0344 421527

SENSITIVE AREAS – MASTER LIST
Derek Belton
Alder House, Whiteleaf, BUCKS HP17 0LQ
Tel: 0844 274475

BRITISH WOMEN PILOTS ASSOCIATION (BWPA)
Rochester Airport, Chatham, KENT ME5 9SD
Tel: 0634 816340

CIVIL AVIATION AUTHORITY

CAA(Gatwick)
Aviation House, Gatwick Airport South, West Sussex RH6 0YR
Tel: 0293 567171

CAA (London)
CAA House, 45–59 Kingsway, LONDON WC2B 6TE
Tel: 071 379 7311

CAA Printing & Publications Services
Greville House, 37 Gratton Road, Cheltenham, Glos. GL50 2BN
Tel: 0242 35151

APPENDIX 4

BBAC EXAMINERS (PPL Balloons)

Ray Bailey
2 Swift Close, Pennyfarthings, Watermead, Aylesbury,
Bucks HP20 2UF
Tel: 0296 398119

Tony Brown
Sudpre Cottage, Worplesdon, Guildford, Surrey
Tel: 0483 233895

Don Cameron
3 The Knoll, Portishead, Bristol BS20 9NU
Tel: 0272 637216 (work)

Tom Donnelly
24 Main Street, Sprotborough, Doncaster DN5 7RF
Tel: 0302 852244

Phil Dunnington
Mulberry House, Front Street, Churchill, BS19 5NB
Tel: 0272 637216 (work)

Chris Kirby
c/o Thunder & Colt, Maesbury Road, Oswestry,
Shropshire SY10 8HA
Tel: 0691 670644

Kevin Meehan
15 Southfield Road, Much Wenlock, Shropshire TF13 6AX
Tel: 0952 292945 (work)

Mike Moore
249 Passage Road, Bristol BS10 7BJ
Tel: 0272 501196

Joe Philp
Addicroft, Upton Cross, Liskeard, Cornwall
Tel: 0579 62208

Laurie Ryan
23 Baldock Road, Letchworth, Herts SG6 3JX
Tel: 04626 683678

Gerry Turnbull
Cymcynfelin, Clyro, Hereford HR3 3SE
Tel: 0497 820169

Crispin Williams
c/o Thunder & Colt, Maesbury Road, Oswestry,
Shropshire SY10 8HA
Tel: 0691 670644

APPENDIX 5

BOOK LIST

Meteorology Simplified	A.O.P.A.
Meteorology for Glider Pilots	C E Wallington
The Weather Guide	A G Forsdyke
Air Pilot's Manual: Volume 2	Trevor Thom
CAP 85 − A guide to aviation law, flight rules and procedures for applicants for the PPL	CAA
CAP 413 — Radio Telephony Procedures	CAA
CAP 494 — British Civil Aviation Requirements — Part 31 — Manned Free Balloons	CAA
Pooley's Flight Guide	R Pooley, W Ryall
Ballooning Handbook	Don Cameron
First Aid Manual	St John Ambulance St Andrews Ambulance Association The British Red Cross Society

INDEX